THE

ELEPHANT'S TRUNK

OTHER BOOKS BY ROBERT J. ADAMS

* * *

THE STUMP FARM

BEYOND THE STUMP FARM

HORSE COP

FISH COP

THE
ELEPHANT'S
TRUNK

ROBERT J. ADAMS

MEGAMY

THE PUBLISHER:
Megamy Publishing Ltd.
P. O. Box 3507
Spruce Grove, Alberta, Canada T7X 3A7
E-mail: megamy@compusmart.ab.ca

Canadian Cataloguing in Publication Data
Adams, Robert J., 1938–
    The elephant's trunk

ISBN 0-9681916-7-3

    1. Adams, Robert J., 1938– —Journeys. 2. Voyages and travels --Humor. I. Title.

G465.A33 2000   910.4'02'07   C99-901375-0

Senior Editor: Kelly Hymanyk
Copy Editor: Natalie King
Design, layout, and production: Kelly Hymanyk
Cover: Rage Studios Inc.
Printing: Jasper Printing

DEDICATION

For Martha. My wife, my friend, and my travelling companion.

CONTENTS

DISCLAIMER

The stories you are about to read are all true. The men, women, and children you will read about are all people from my past. I have taken the liberty of changing the names of many of them to protect their identities. Although I view the past as being very humorous, they may not.

ACKNOWLEDGEMENTS

Holidays, or adventures, such as Mar and I are prone to take have been enhanced and made far more enjoyable by the many wonderful people and characters that we have been fortunate enough to share them with. The people we have met in our travels are far too numerous to mention. Many of these individuals have shared one holiday or a portion of a holiday. Others we have travelled with many times.

There are many wonderful memories of holidays shared with Dale Fayram and Lois Fayram, the two people who I believe must share the responsibility for our globetrotting habits. There has never been a dull moment with Lester and Rose Wall; we have shared with them friendship, companionship, and gut-bustin' laughter, more than with any others, on numerous holidays, at home and abroad. We have had the privilege and pleasure of holidaying from Mexico to Alaska with Donald (Captain Don T.) and Joan Tetzlaff.

To the many other people whose paths we crossed, some for a very short time, thanks for many varied and fabulous memories. Some of these individuals, although I have not named them, or have used a fictitious name, appear on the pages in this book.

INTRODUCTION

Adams continues to engross readers young and old with his engaging charm and inspiring humour in *The Elephant's Trunk*. Journey with Adams throughout the world, laugh with him as he continues to find humour in his travels with family, friends, and acquaintances.

Enjoy Adams living life to the fullest, while he confirms for us through humour that a good vacation makes us laugh and creates life's memorable moments.

MEGAMY PUBLISHING

THE

ELEPHANT'S TRUNK

THE WHITE PRINCESS

"Be very careful," cautioned the African behind the counter at the car-rental agency in Harare, Zimbabwe. "My people are very poor, and to them, you are very rich," he added. The man was going to great lengths to make sure I was well aware that my life was not in peril, but my belongings certainly were.

"Well," I replied wearily. "Your people may be very poor, but I can assure you, sir, that I am anything but rich."

"To my people, you are rich," he replied emphatically, shaking a finger at me to drive home his point. "Very, very rich."

"Thanks. I'll remember that."

"Please, sir, remember to guard your possessions at all times. My people will steal them if they get a chance."

"Thanks again," I replied, forcing myself to stay awake while I smiled. "I'll be sure to guard my possessions. At all times."

This was my first conversation on arriving, with Mar, in Zimbabwe to start our five-week African holiday. It was not much of a welcome. After close to fifty hours in airports and on airplanes, what I needed more than anything was sleep. I could easily have forgone the welcoming committee for a bed.

"One more thing," cautioned the African as he held out a set of keys for the vehicle that would be our transportation for the next five weeks: "If you should get a flat tire, sir, do not stop your car."

"What?" I asked, leaning heavily on the counter, half asleep, wondering if I was in fact dreaming this conversation. "You don't want me to change the tire?"

"No, sir. Do not stop the car," he replied, and his eyes grew wide.

"Why not, doesn't the car have a spare tire?" I mumbled drowsily.

"Oh yes, sir," he replied, nodding his head up and down. "It has a spare tire. But I caution you, do not stop the car. Many of my people will see that you have a flat tire, and they will yell at you, 'Master, stop the car! You have a flat tire, master!' But do not stop the car. They want to steal your belongings."

"What do I do with the flat tire?" I asked. "Do you mean you want me to drive on the rim?"

"Yes, sir," he replied. "You will drive on the rim. You will keep driving until you find a big tourist hotel. Turn into the hotel and stop at the front door. Ask the man at the door for help, and he will help you change the tire."

"I don't know why I just don't stop and change it," I replied, "but, whatever, right now I just want to find a bed."

"Because, sir, my people will come to help you. Then they will take all of your suitcases out of the car and put them on the road, and when one is helping you change the flat tire, my people will steal all your luggage. My people won't hurt you, sir, but my people, they are very poor and you are very rich. They would be very rich too, if they were to steal all your luggage and have all your nice clothes."

"Thanks again," I replied. "I'll remember that, if I should have a flat tire."

"Please, sir, remember that," he said. "My people are very poor."

"Okay, okay," I replied. "Just tell me where I find the car."

"It's outside, sir, in the parking lot," he replied with a big smile. "Just ask the man outside for your car. Tell him you want the White Princess."

"The what?" I asked.

"The White Princess," he laughed. "It is a very nice little car. You will be very happy with it."

I handed Mar the keys to the White Princess, then I assumed my normal holiday role as Pack Mule Bob. The guy who had just rented me the White Princess smiled as I struggled to pick up all our baggage. His smile widened as I hoisted piece after piece up onto my arms, my shoulders, and my back. Out the front doors I wobbled after Mar, who was weighed down by the keys to the White Princess. Mar was more than ten steps ahead of me and pulling away. She cleared the road and was over in the parking lot looking for the attendant by the time I cleared the sidewalk.

"Can I see your contract?" the man asked.

"We're looking for the White Princess," I gasped as I caught up with Mar and the attendant.

"They are all white princesses, sir," the man informed us. "Could I see your contract, please?"

"Show him the keys, Mar," I said. The contract was securely stowed in one of my pockets, and I didn't really relish the thought of unloading my pack until I saw the White Princess.

"I need your contract, sir," the man repeated.

"Where's the contract?" Mar asked.

"I don't know," I moaned. "It's got to be in one of my pockets. Can't you just take the licence number off the keys?"

"I need to see your contract," he repeated.

So our holiday in Africa began in a rent-a-car parking lot with Mar searching through the pockets of Pack Mule Bob, trying to find the contract.

"Follow me," he said when Mar finally produced the paper, and he led us over to a small white car.

"This is it?" Mar laughed. "This is the White Princess? This is what we're going to drive around Africa in?"

I looked at the man. He was grinning and nodding his head.

"It looks like this is it, all right," I replied as I began

to unburden myself of the luggage. Mar and I both stood there looking at the White Princess. A well-used princess. Dents and scratches covered the entire body. Streaks of orange rust leaked from the scrapes, streaking and bubbling the white paint.

"Check the tires, will you?" I asked Mar. "I want to make sure there are no flats before we drive out of here."

"I'd say the tires are the least of your worries," she replied. I think she would have laughed again, but she was just too tired.

A walk around the car pretty well confirmed her impression. I had to agree, the tires were the least of my worries.

"Do you think it will start?" she asked.

"Should we try it before or after we load our luggage?" I kidded her.

The door squeaked a welcome. The hinges had not felt a drop of oil in some time. I was pleasantly surprised when, with a twist of the key, the little motor purred like a kitten.

"Well," I said as I got out of the car, "the motor certainly sounds good. Now I could use some sleep. Let's get this thing loaded and get to the hotel."

"Can you get everything in the trunk?" Mar asked.

"I don't know," I mumbled, jostling suitcases and bags, trying to find the winning combination.

The airport in Harare was about five miles out of the city. A friend back home had given me a map of the city, and I had taken the liberty of tracing out our route. Mar was to be the navigator on our African adventure.

Now, in all fairness to her, Mar is not the best navigator in the world, and after two days in the air and in airports, a very tired Mar was about to put her navigational skills to the supreme test. She had to get us through the streets of Harare to our hotel. Thankfully, this was a leisurely vacation. We had five weeks to get out and see the country, or find our hotel. Our only real commitment was to be back at the airport in time to catch the return flight home. I gave Mar the map of the city and showed her our route. The map was well used; it showed the wear and tear of being folded and unfolded many times. It was a delicate thing, but I hoped there was at least one more trip in those tired old folds.

The only thing on my mind when I pulled out onto the highway was how good that bed was going to feel. I think Mar shared my thoughts, from the way she snuggled down in the seat. It looked suspiciously as if my navigator was going to fall asleep at any second. There was little traffic, and I quickly pulled over into my lane and headed for the city, the hotel, and a bed.

"Get over on your own side of the road!" she yelled excitedly. She scared about ten years off my life expectancy. Mar wasn't nearly as sleepy as I had thought.

"I am . . . " I started to argue, but the vehicle heading straight for the White Princess helped to remind me that in Zimbabwe, they drive on the wrong side of the road. Suddenly, my heart was beating like a trip-hammer as I herded the White Princess over to the left side of the road. I nearly missed hitting a large truck head-on.

Surprisingly, that truck wasn't the least bit intimidated by the White Princess.

After that little jolt, I was wide awake. I drove a fair distance without any other life-threatening incident, and I was lulled back to a sense of false security. I was in a nice drowsy stage by the time we reached the city limits.

Then, the unthinkable happened.

In a dreamlike state, I heard *whappa, whappa, whappa*—a sound like flopping rubber hitting the hardtop. The tar road seemed to have got a little rough, and from somewhere afar a voice called to me: "Master! Master!"

"Master! Stop, master! You've got a flat tire, master!" came the voice. Even above the sound of a metal rim on a tar road, the voice was loud and clear.

"What's that noise?" Mar asked.

"Would you believe it?" I snapped. "We've got a bloody flat tire."

"No!" she exclaimed, and I could see the concern in her eyes.

Instinctively, my foot left the gas pedal and slammed on the brake. The White Princess ground to a halt. Then I remembered the warning I had taken so lightly. I looked in the rear-view mirror. A lone African was racing down the road towards the White Princess and our precious baggage. Instinctively, as fear gripped me, my foot left the brake and I tramped the gas pedal to the floor. *Whappa, whappa, whappa.* The sound of rubber slapping on the tar road got louder and the tempo picked up.

The sound of rubber slapping the tar road had attracted attention. In the rear-view mirror, I could see that the lone African now had company: several Africans were chasing after the White Princess. Down the highway we sped. Down the highway raced the Africans. They were running as fast as their legs would carry them. Much to my horror, I realized that some of those legs could run about as fast as the White Princess was going. The lone African, the first to holler, was leading the pack and he was gaining on me. Would he be the first to reach the little White Princess and its cargo of luggage?

Now was the time to panic. Now I needed a navigator. I was glad that I had taken the time to trace out the route to our hotel.

"We gotta turn, up here somewhere!" I yelled at Mar. "What street do we turn on?"

"I'm looking," she replied.

"Well, look harder!" I yelled at her. "We've got to get to that hotel before that horde of Africans gets to us."

I glanced at Mar and the map. My heart skipped a beat when I realized my yelling hadn't helped either Mar or the map. Where once we had a map with folds, we now had four maps. As I sped through the streets of Harare, Mar was busy trying to piece them together. I had a sinking feeling that neither the navigator nor the map were going to be of any help trying to find the hotel. The four pieces refused to fit back together in the same order. We drove along blindly, praying for a hotel. Any hotel.

As we drove deeper into the city, the calls increased in number and volume.

"Master! Master! You've got a flat tire!" came the cries of many voices. Now people were pointing at the rear tire from the sidewalks. Many more Africans left their posts, where they had been leaning against buildings, and raced onto the street. The White Princess was a very popular gal; she was gathering quite a following.

I took another look in the rear-view mirror. The first guy who had called out to inform me of the flat tire was still hot on my tail. That was one persistent man. Suddenly it dawned on me.

"See that guy in the lead?" I barked at Mar. "He's the first guy that chased us. I'll bet he waits out on that bloody highway for a tourist with a flat, and then runs him into the ground and steals his baggage." I could swear that he was gaining on the White Princess. I was really beginning to worry, and to sweat. With the horde of Africans chasing after the White Princess, I was beginning to worry about my life, not my baggage. A multitude of Africans, young and old, raced after the White Princess. They were all pointing at the rear tire. They were all trying to catch the stupid white man who didn't know he had a flat tire. *Whappa, whappa, whappa. Thump, thump, thump.* There was a new sound as the rubber slapped both the hardtop and the fender well.

"Stop! Stop!" Mar suddenly screamed, dropping the four pieces of the Harare map on the floor. "Red light. Red light!"

"Where?" I yelled, and I hit the binders. I had been so intent on watching the gathering mob in the rear-view mirror that I forgot we were in the city. Traffic lights were the last thing on my mind. The White Princess whapped and thumped to a halt in the middle of the intersection. I looked over to the side of the road, but didn't see any light, red or otherwise. Suddenly, horns were blaring, adding a new tone to the symphony that surrounded the White Princess.

"I don't see any lights," I snapped. I was staring at the right-hand side of the street.

"There, right over there. Can't you see it?" she said and pointed to the left side of the road. "On the left side, Bob, look on the *left* side of the road."

"I forgot," I reluctantly admitted. "Everything's backwards over here."

"Master! Master! You've got a flat tire!" The screaming was getting louder. I took another look in the rear-view mirror. Man, those Africans were getting mighty close. I gunned the motor, and the White Princess lurched. Then she coughed. She stopped, then jumped. I thought she was going to stall, but she caught and, finally, we jerked through the intersection and the red light.

"I know one thing for sure," I mumbled to Mar. "This is no place for a sleep-starved man to be driving, with or without a flat tire."

I looked in the rear-view mirror once more. But the red light and traffic had not deterred the mob. The cars that had stopped for the White Princess were still in the intersection, and the African horde, led by the persistent man, hadn't hesitated. They had raced through the intersection and the red light.

"I'll tell you another thing, Mar," I muttered as I pressed down on the gas pedal. "If this is what Africa is like, they can keep it." At every building and street corner we passed, more people jumped to their feet. They would point at the flat tire and the obviously-deaf white man driving the car. Then they would shout and wave and race into the street to join the many others who were trying to tell the deaf white man of his plight.

"There's a hotel!" Mar suddenly yelled, and pointed to a welcome sight on the opposite side of the road. Not only was it a hotel, it was a major hotel, with a beautiful drive, and it was off the street.

I cut in front of an oncoming car, and as fast as the White Princess could go, I raced into the drive. Up the ramp I drove and stopped right in front of the huge main doors and the doorman. He was a sight to behold, decked out like a brigadier general in ceremonial dress. He stood ramrod-straight. A no-nonsense type of guy. My type of guy.

The doorman marched over to the passenger side and opened the door for Mar to exit. Then he started around to my side, but I beat him to the draw. I flung open the door and gave the startled man, surely a saviour in the face of the horde, a big bear hug.

"Did you know you have a flat tire, sir?" asked the somewhat embarrassed man in a very serious tone.

"Yeah, I know," I replied. "That's why I pulled in here. I need to have it changed."

"Are you staying at the hotel, sir?" he asked.

"I wish I was," I replied, "but I'm not. Look, I'm dead tired, and all I need is to have the tire changed and I'll be on my way. Can you do that for me?"

"I'm sorry, sir," he replied, "but you cannot stay here. You are blocking the drive for our guests. You will have to move your car."

"Right. But there's nobody here. I'll move the car just as soon as you change my tire. I'll get out of your driveway and be on my way."

"Very well, sir. If you'll just follow me, I'll get someone to change your tire," he replied rather curtly.

He started to walk down the drive, and I followed, as requested, walking right along behind him. He only took a couple of steps before he stopped.

"Please, sir. Would you follow me in your car? You cannot leave your car parked here."

"Okay, right," I replied and got back into my car and followed him down the drive. Out onto the street I drove. Out to the many, many Africans. Africans who had just finished chasing me through the streets of Harare.

The doorman stopped and held up his hand. I slammed on the brakes. Lucky for him, I also stopped. If I hadn't, the hotel would have been short one doorman. He looked around at the crowd of Africans who had circled the White Princess, and called to one of them. The man who had originally chased us through the streets of Harare stepped forward with a big grin on his face.

"This man will change your tire for you, sir," he declared.

"But the spare tire's in the trunk."

"I certainly hope so," he replied. "If not, you won't get your flat tire changed."

"But . . . he'll have to take my luggage out of the trunk and put it on the street," I protested.

"That's right, sir. He'll have to take your luggage out of the trunk and put it on the street. Then he can take the spare tire out of the trunk and put it on your car. That is, if you want your tire changed."

I nodded. The doorman gave the signal, and the man changed the tire and, much to my surprise and relief, placed the flat as well as my luggage back in the trunk.

"You should pay the man for changing your flat tire," the doorman said. He had stayed there, right beside the White Princess, standing as erect as a flagpole, staring off at some distant point.

"Right," I replied. "How much would you like?" I asked the man who had just changed the tire.

"Whatever you think it's worth, Master," he replied, shrugging his shoulders and avoiding eye contact.

I took out my wallet and searched through the bills. I extracted one and handed it to the man.

"I hope this is enough," I said.

"Thank you, master," replied the happy man. He was grinning from ear to ear. Then he turned and faced the horde. His smile faded and, clutching the bill, he bolted. He charged down the street, past the horde. He was running as if his life depended on it, like a gazelle being chased by a pride of hungry lions. The horde, moving as one, was hot on his heels.

I looked at the doorman for his approval, hoping that I had paid the man enough. The doorman's eyes were about the size of saucers.

"Sir . . . sir," he stammered, "you just gave that man almost a full week's wages!"

"Five dollars. I only gave the man five dollars," I mumbled to Mar as I looked back into my wallet and thumbed through the contents, a few ones, some fives, tens and a twenty. Altogether I had about a hundred bucks.

"In their eyes I must be a very, very rich man."

TRIP OF A LIFETIME

A pack trip into Willmore Wilderness Park, located on the north boundary of Jasper National Park, has to be the highlight of any outdoorsman's life. This is a trip of a lifetime. Non government motor vehicles are prohibited, so the mode of transportation is foot or horseback.

On numerous occasions in the past, I had travelled into Willmore Wilderness Park, but usually it was work-related in one way or another. Now, after months of careful planning, I was about to embark on the trip of a lifetime.

Normally, my travelling companions were my brother, my Dad, or long-time friends — people I knew well and had travelled with in the past. No surprises. I don't particularly like surprises, certainly not when I'm back in the bush. On this trip, however, I had a new companion. A chap I had just met. He was a keener, and as eager as I for a holiday in the Rockies. He had a considerable amount of travel experience and assured me he was an expert horseman.

"I have a way with horses," he warbled. "When I get in the saddle, I lean forward and whisper in their ears. Yes sir, we understand each other real well."

In the short time that I had known him, I had seen enough to know that most of what he talked about, he could back up.

When I had told Mom of my trip, she immediately gave me the third degree. I can still hear her voice as I was going over the last-minute details.

"You should be going on a trip like this with your brother or your father," she scolded. "You know nothing about this person. You could get yourself killed." Mom was a little suspicious of people she didn't know very well. Mom was also a firm believer that once-in-a-lifetime trips like this should be shared with those closest to you.

"You worry too much, Mom," I kidded her.

My new-found partner and I had put our heads together and planned every little detail. Man, but he was a stickler for detail. For a while, I thought that he was even going to count the matches. Now we were conducting our final check: cameras; film; binoculars; spotting scope; and grub, each meal planned down to the last tea bag. In fact, we had even divided the cooking chores. My partner would cook breakfast.

"Don't worry," he crowed. "I'm an expert. I cook a mean spread of bacon and eggs over an open fire. I'll have you drooling all over yourself," he laughed.

Lunch would be sandwiches on the trail, and I would cook supper. I made no such brash statement about my cooking, for I had tasted some of it in the past.

The horses had been contracted from a local outfitter, and for this trip we had splurged — we were taking a wrangler. A wrangler was a luxury beyond my wildest dreams, not to mention my pocketbook. But what the heck, this was, after all, the trip of a lifetime. There would be no hassles with the horses. No getting up early and chasing them through brush hanging heavy with dew. In addition to the horses, the outfitter was supplying all the tack, tent, cooking utensils, and camp stove. Why, this trip would have all the comforts of home.

We left Hinton, driving west on Highway 16 to the Forestry Trunk Road, and turned north. We crossed the Athabasca River on the old railway trestle, now a one-way vehicle bridge, and continued along the old right-of-way to the Entrance Ranger Station. To get to Rock Lake, we had decided to use the back road. We travelled west past the ranger station, along the north bank of the Athabasca River towards Brûlé. In the early morning sun, the Rocky Mountains had a pinkish hue to them.

"Looks like we got ourselves a good day to travel," I commented to my partner as we crossed the height of land, before dropping down to Solomon Creek.

The road followed Solomon Creek through the valley on the east side of the Boule Range, and then cut north. We snaked through spruce and pine forest, past open meadows; we crossed Ice Water Creek and Wildhay River. Joining up with the main road, we followed the Wildhay to Rock Lake.

29

The staging area was nestled in the trees just east of the Rock Lake Ranger Station. There were mountains on all sides. Everywhere we looked, there were mountains. We arrived just after dawn, and it truly was a glorious fall morning in the Canadian Rockies. The sun was shining. The sky was a clear, deep blue. There was not a cloud to be seen. It was early morning, but already it was warm enough that jackets were not necessary.

I looked at the horses: three were tied to trees, and half a dozen more were tied to the corral railings. The outfitter and, I suspected, the wrangler were busy getting the pack saddles onto the horses tethered to the railing.

I smiled to myself. The trip of a lifetime was off to a perfect start. I could barely contain my excitement as I envisioned the next six days, roaming mountains that were bathed in sunlight. Drinking pure, fresh water from the streams and springs that were so common throughout the area. Ah, yes, it was a perfect world. I sat there, enjoying my good fortune and congratulating myself on this brilliant idea.

Having a wrangler meant that I had little to do until the horses were packed. My partner and I sat back in the truck and enjoyed the moment. My mind wandered as I thought of all the outfitters who hunted and packed into the south end of the Willmore Wilderness Park. Although Willmore is a park, hunting is allowed within its borders. Otherwise, there is little to separate it from Jasper National Park.

In the 1960s and 1970s, except for the outfitters and hunters in the fall, there was very little human activity in the park. Even during the hunting season, the height of activity, one rarely encounters another human being in the vastness of the Willmore. It is truly a wilderness experience. Very few people took advantage of the great outdoor experiences the park has to offer. Ah, yes, the trip of a lifetime, alone, almost, in the heart of the Rockies.

The park's serene natural beauty is breathtaking. Who would ever forget the cheerful song of the mountain chickadee flitting among the spruce; the throaty call of the raven gliding above the treetops; the chatter of the red squirrel scolding an intruder; the whispering of the wind caressing the top of the trees; or the water from one of many small streams bubbling and gurgling over the rocks as it begins its journey to the Arctic Ocean? Who would not be moved by the sight of a snow-white cloud forming a halo near the top of a mountain peak, or by the wispy tendrils of clouds being whipped over a mountain crest?

As I relaxed, I glanced towards the corral, looking at the pack horses. Another animal had suddenly materialized among the pack animals. My jaw dropped in disbelief.

"See anything that looks like it doesn't belong?" I asked my partner, the expert horseman.

He looked over the staging area, the corrals, the horses, the tack, the outfitter, and the wrangler. "Looks fine to me," he said.

"Have another look. How many heads, tails, and feet do you count?" I asked.

My partner diligently counted and proudly proclaimed that we had a tail for each head. But there seemed to be an extra set of legs. The legs tallied up to the exact number of animals we had contracted, but we seemed to be short a head and tail set.

We got out of the truck for a closer examination of the horses.

"What is this supposed to be, camp meat?" I asked the outfitter, pointing to a little pinto-coloured horse that came up to about the bellies of the other horses.

"That's Shorty. He's going with you on the trail. He's one of your pack horses."

"You're kidding me, right?" I asked in disbelief.

"Don't knock Shorty. He's a good little pack horse," the outfitter snarled. Then he patted Shorty on the withers; that is, he sort of leaned over and patted him on the withers.

"Who you trying to convince, me or you?" I said rather sarcastically, walking over to have a better look at Shorty. Standing next to him, I quickly realized that I had to look down to see the top of his head.

"So, tell me, what is it that Shorty packs, lunch?" I asked.

"Don't worry about him. He'll pull his weight," replied the outfitter defensively.

"I'm not worried about his weight," I stated. "This isn't a kiddies' ride. We need good pack horses and that's what I ordered, good pack horses. I think I'm getting shortchanged here." I looked down at Shorty's stumpy little legs. "Look at his little legs—he won't be able to get over a deadfall even if it's lying flat on the ground, and with the pack on he won't be able to get under one either."

"Shorty's a good pack horse, I use him all the time on the trail. You wait and see."

"If you ask me, Shorty should have little rockers put on his little hoofs, and you should take his little carcass to a little circus where little kids can rock back and forth on the little mother."

"Well, I'm not asking you," he snapped at me, "and it's a good thing too, else I'da lost me a good pack horse a long time ago."

"I don't know," I said. "I don't like it. I'd just as soon not have to find out anything on the trail. Shorty doesn't appear to me to be much of a pack horse. In fact, he doesn't appear to be much of a horse, period. Looks to me like we're only getting half a horse when we contracted for a full horse. I'd say half a horse is only worth half the price, if he's worth that. Wouldn't you say so?" I asked my partner, who immediately backed me up by not saying anything. He just stood there, with a grin on his face, looking at the pint-sized horse.

The outfitter and the wrangler finished putting pack saddles on the horses at the railing. Including Shorty. Then, while the wrangler saddled the three riding horses, the outfitter and I sorted out the gear for the panniers. The weight had to be distributed evenly so that the saddle didn't shift and fall to one side, ending up under the horse's belly. "Look out for a rodeo if that happens," said the outfitter.

A disturbance over by the saddle horses caught our attention. I looked up in time to see my partner, the expert horseman, trying to mount the horse he would share the trip with. His horse was standing in the middle of the staging area, and he was furiously scrambling into the saddle. With both hands clasped firmly on the saddle horn he leaned forward towards the horse's head.

"Whoa horsey. Whoa. Whoa horsey," he cooed gently.

I looked over at the outfitter. He was standing there with his mouth open, not really believing what he was seeing.

"My partner has a way with horses," I informed the surprised man. "I believe 'whoa horsey' is the way he establishes contact with the animal."

My partner probably should have leaned a little closer to the horse's ear and whispered a little louder. Almost immediately it appeared that he had not made the necessary contact to cement the bond between man and animal. As we watched, the horse stretched his neck out and down. The reins slipped through my partner's hands. When the horse had its head, it started to walk slowly out of the staging area. My partner was beginning to sound a little more desperate, and he clutched the saddle horn with both hands as he tried desperately to make contact with his horse.

"Whoa horsey. Whoa," he called out in a voice that was certainly above a whisper. We heard him repeat the words again and again. His knuckles on the saddle horn turned white and he spoke louder still, but not so loud as to spook the animal. The trusty steed walked around the south side of the corrals, the expert horseman hanging on for dear life.

We could hear the snapping and cracking of twigs and branches as the horse walked into the brush and out of sight. The sounds abated as the horse got farther and farther away. Above the cracking and snapping of timber, my partner could still be heard trying to communicate with the horse.

"Whoa horsey. Whoa. Whoa horsey," he repeated continuously until his voice faded in the distance.

"What'd you do, give him a deaf horse?" I asked the outfitter, who just shrugged his shoulders. He was used to greenhorns on the trail.

"That's Thunder, he's just goin' for a drink down at the crick," he said matter-of-factly and went back to packing the boxes. "Thunder just wants to see who's boss. It happens all the time," he said, showing absolutely no concern for my partner, the expert horseman. Before too long, the sound of an animal plowing through the brush could once again be heard, and the words "Whoa horsey, whoa" got louder and louder as Thunder walked out of the brush and back into the staging area. There he stopped. My partner, the expert horseman, must have finally made contact, or else Thunder just got tired and stopped to rest. My partner and Thunder stayed right in the middle of the staging area, and there they waited for the trip to commence.

True to his word, the outfitter left the pack saddle on Shorty, balanced two panniers, one on either side, placed some of the larger equipment on top of the panniers, covered everything with a tarp, threw a diamond hitch on the works, and cinched everything down tight.

Shorty no longer looked like a small horse. Now he looked like a tarp with a horse's head sticking out one end and a tail out the other. The bottom of the pack was only slightly above the ground — and that was beside the corral where the ground was level.

"Will it move," I asked the outfitter, "or is the corral holding him up?" Shorty looked like he might be a little over-packed for the occasion.

"I told you, he's fine," the outfitter assured us. "Shorty's a good pack horse. I use him all the time."

"Yeah, so you keep telling us. Well, you better hope you're right," I said, "because if he doesn't perform, I'm deducting him from the final payment."

"You gonna tie them horses together?" I asked, noticing each pack horse had a free rein.

"No need," he said, pointing to the wrangler. "You take the lead and make sure that one of your riders brings up the rear. These horses trail real good once you get 'em going, no need to tie them. They'll just follow the lead horse." With those words of encouragement, we were off to enjoy the trip of a lifetime in Willmore Wilderness Park.

There was not a single cloud in the sky as we mounted our horses.

We trailed past the ranger station that was located on the northeast shore of Rock Lake. I had often commented on the view the ranger had from his living room, looking south across Rock Lake towards the Jasper Park boundary.

Leaving Rock Lake, we followed the trail along the Wildhay River, up the valley that separates the Persimmon and the Berland ranges.

The trail into the Willmore is actually a road that Forestry maintains in the summer and is easily passable by car if one has a key to get past the gate at the Willmore boundary. I had taken my car in there on numerous trips, checking hunters and outfitters. We took the horse path around the gate and walked on. Arriving at the ford on the Wildhay River, we stopped to water our horses.

"That's the Rock Lake fire tower," I informed my buddy and pointed to the buildings sitting on a height of land towards Daybreak Peak south of us.

It was turning out to be a hot fall day, shirt-sleeve weather. Our jackets were tied behind the saddle along with our rain gear, and I was thinking, if it weren't for the wasps that were constantly buzzing around the horses, I'd take my shirt off too.

To my surprise, Shorty was actually holding his own. Although his little legs were taking two steps to every one of the other horses, he was moving right along. The wrangler was still at the head of the pack, and I brought up the rear.

My partner, on the other hand, was sometimes right behind the leader, sometimes just in front of me. Sometimes he was behind me, and sometimes he was in the middle of the pack train. Sometimes he and Thunder would just walk off by themselves. It had been decided back at the staging area who the boss was, and the boss decided where they would be in the pack train.

The expert horseman rode wherever Thunder decided to take him. We passed Seep Creek and Carson Creek, as well as numerous small springs. Thunder considered each his own watering hole and stopped at every one to drink and gaze around the countryside.

We never met another soul on the trail. It was as if we were alone on the planet, under the bluest of skies with not a hint of a breeze. It was a perfect day to be in the Willmore. It was a perfect day to be alive. Let my partner go wherever Thunder decided, I was enjoying the perfect trip at the end of the pack train.

At the Eagles Nest cabin the trail forked, the left fork crossing the Wildhay and heading south, following Eagles Nest Creek through Eagles Nest Pass. The right fork continued up the valley along the Wildhay towards the headwaters of the Berland River. We took the left fork, heading south into Eagles Nest Pass, which actually divides the Persimmon Range in two.

There was lots of daylight left. There was no need to push the horses; it would be an easy ride through the pass. We would camp on the west side of the pass at one of the many campsites established and maintained by outfitters.

Although we had been in and along the mountains since we crossed the height of land on Solomon Creek Peak near Brûlé, it is in Eagles Nest Pass where one gets the true feeling of the Canadian Rockies. On both sides of the trail the mountains tower overhead, the small pockets of snow and ice adding depth and colour to their grandeur. The trail had been chiselled out of the side of the mountain. In many places you can reach out and actually touch the rocks of the mountain while remaining seated in the saddle. The trail winds along Eagles Nest Creek, along the valley floor, up over a high spot before snaking back down again. A different scene at every turn.

We were well into the pass and had just climbed a fairly steep hill where the trail had been cut along the side of the mountain. I was sitting back in the saddle, lost in my dreams, enjoying the day and the scenery. To the right the mountain went straight up. To the left were a few pine trees scattered about on fifteen feet of steep-sloping hillside, and then an abrupt drop of about two hundred feet to the bottom of the canyon and the creek below.

It was here, on the first day of the trip of a lifetime, that Shorty decided he'd had enough of the horse's tail in front of him. He was clearly bored with walking along the road, where both he and his pack found little resistance. The biggest obstacles were small rocks about the size of Texas pea gravel that he hardly had to lift a hoof to clear. Shorty decided that it was time to make his move; he was about to show us his best imitation of a mountain goat. We had been lulled into a false sense of security by the calm and quiet of the day.

Suddenly, without any warning, Shorty bolted from the pack train. Farting and snorting, he turned right and went straight up the side of the mountain. The horse immediately behind him turned and, with absolutely no hesitation whatsoever, followed Shorty. Before we realized what was happening, we had three pack horses heading up the side of the mountain, Shorty in the lead.

39

It was more good luck than good management, the next horse in line just happened to be Thunder, with my partner on his back. Oblivious to the changing world around them, Thunder and the expert horseman continued along the trail as if nothing had happened. They were in a world of their own, as they walked on and out of sight.

The rest of the pack train stayed on the trail, some standing, some walking, some trailing after the expert horseman. The wrangler took a bead on Shorty and gave chase. He registered his displeasure by cussing out both the outfitter and Shorty as he spurred his horse up the side of the mountain. I sat on my horse and watched. Could this be the rodeo the outfitter had mentioned earlier in the day?

The two horses following Shorty were having some difficulty trying to climb through the trees with their packs. But it was nothing compared to what Shorty was experiencing. Stumpy little legs pumping, nostrils flared, and farting prolifically, Shorty plowed on. Pack boxes were slamming against stumps, rocks, deadfall, and of course, the standing trees. But Shorty was undeterred. Every time he ran into one obstacle he would kick, jump, snort, and fart until he was free. Then he would head for the next obstacle. I had to hand it to Shorty, he was a determined little cuss.

The two horses following Shorty stopped when their packs got snagged on a tree, and the wrangler was able to get them with no trouble and bring them back to the trail, but Shorty was a different matter. He was a challenge. He was headed for the top of the mountain just a-snortin' and a-blowin' while clawing for better footing. I'm not certain if it was more the cussin' and swearin' on the part of the wrangler, who was once again hot on Shorty's trail, or the difficulty of the climb that finally got Shorty turned around and headed down again.

Coming down the mountain didn't sound or look like it was any easier for Shorty. His metal shoes slamming into the rocks made quite a racket, second only to the sound of the packs banging and grinding into rock and wood. As Shorty burst through the timber, his pack had slipped and was hanging precariously on his left side. I expected at any moment to see it turn completely under his belly. Not a bad idea, I thought; that would at least high-centre the little cayuse.

Yes, this was the rodeo the outfitter had predicted.

In the past, I had participated in several searches for persons lost in the bush, and I know for a fact that they will cross a road without realizing it was there. I'm not sure if Shorty was lost or just determined to get to the bottom of the mountain, but he never even hesitated when he got to the trail. With the pack hanging to one side, fartin' and snortin' like a steam engine, Shorty charged across the trail and started through the trees on the other side.

Shorty covered the fifteen feet between the trail and the cliff in nothing flat. The creek was a couple of hundred feet below the trees and the rim. I had a sinking feeling that we were about to lose everything that was hanging on the side of Shorty. In a blind charge, he was heading for disaster.

But Shorty was not as blind as I thought. Arriving at the cliff he suddenly veered to the right and ran along the edge, his pack hanging out over thin air. Shorty was charging along a mighty thin line as the pack bounced with his every step. There were times when I swear his feet would leave the ground, but the gutsy little horse managed to claw back and get a hoof-hold on the rocks. He continued to run along the edge of that cliff, dodging every tree to the thin-air side, thus avoiding having the pack slam into one of them. He was doing a magnificent job.

"Go grab his bridle! He's gonna fall off the cliff," yelled the wrangler, who was still partway up the mountain. He was picking his way down much more gingerly than Shorty had.

"Go grab him yourself. He's not my horse," I yelled back at him, eyeing the steep terrain that led to the drop-off. "But I think you're right. I think he's going to fall off the cliff." I had no doubt that Shorty, the 'good little pack horse', was soon to meet his maker, and I had no intentions of joining him. I congratulated myself on having had the foresight to take a wrangler; the horses were his job.

Shorty soon tired of his tightrope walk, but he had not lost any of his steam. Nostrils still flared and eyes flashing wildly, he turned right and with a hearty fart and a mighty snort, he started back up the mountain. This time the wrangler, no braver than I was about walking the thin line of disaster along the edge of the cliff, was waiting when Shorty hit the trail. As Shorty raced by, he managed to snag onto his bridle and rein him in before he could get across the trail again.

The rodeo was over. Once more, peace and quiet engulfed the pass.

Shorty was in the middle of the trail trying to stand up, but the pack hanging on his side kept dragging him over. Several times it looked as though gravity would intervene and drag him to the ground, but Shorty was a gutsy little guy. He held firm. Shorty looked like a character out of a comic strip, standing there with everything hanging almost under his belly, his nostrils flared and his sides heaving. He would have to be repacked before he could proceed.

"We'll go on ahead and get camp started while you repack that little mother," I told the wrangler. "You can follow up as soon as you've finished. There's a couple of campsites just when you clear through the pass. We'll make camp at the first available one. See you when you get there. Oh, you and Shorty have a good time now!" I gave him my heartiest smile and a good throaty laugh, just to let him know there were no hard feelings about the pint-size horse. I rode on. Nothing was going to put a damper on my trip of a lifetime.

I took the two pack horses that were standing on the trail and continued on, following in the footsteps of Thunder the boss horse, my partner, and the rest of our pack train. I caught up to them within a half a mile. Thunder and my partner were in a familiar position in the line, behind one of the pack horses.

The first campsite, just barely through the pass, was vacant. It was a good campsite, on the side of the mountain, treed and with a nice flat area for the tent. I turned my horse into the campsite. It was still early, but this would be home for the night. The rest of the pack train followed suit, including the expert horseman and his trusty steed.

Unpacking and picketing horses was certainly not in my job description. It was the wrangler's job, but only the Lord knew where he and Shorty had got to. Since the pack horses and I were all in camp, I tied my horse to a tree and began the task of unpacking.

"Whoa horsey, whoa," cooed my partner to his horse as the first panniers hit the ground.

This was to be my trip of a lifetime. I had someone else along who was going to do the grunt work. Why, then, was I whistling and singing as I pulled packs and saddles off horses? Because it was good to be alive and in the mountains on such a beautiful day. It would take more than one little setback to ruin my trip.

"Whoa horsey, nice horsey," whispered my partner tenderly as he patted his horse on the neck. His horse stood patiently by a tree and waited to be relieved of its burden.

"You can get down and help me with the tent," I mentioned to him. "It should be on one of the packs." He responded by sitting in the saddle, where he continued to bond with his horse. I realized that it wasn't really his job either.

"Whoa horsey, whoa," he cooed gently to the standing animal.

The weather was holding, as gorgeous as it had been all day. On the west side of the pass, we were getting the added advantage of the afternoon sun.

Finally, my partner managed to summon up the courage to leave his saddle and separate himself from his mount. He helped me set up the tent and then, to my surprise, volunteered to start a fire and get supper going.

"Whoa up a minute there, partner," I said to him. "Supper's my baby, remember? Anyway, you've had a pretty rough day, so just sit back and relax while I tend to supper."

"Okay," he replied happily, "but, while you're finishing up with the horses, I'll start the fire anyway. Where's the stove?"

"All right," I relented. "I haven't found the stove yet. You'll have to rustle around in the packs and find it."

When I finished with the horses and came back into the camp, my partner had a nice fire going in the firepit. I looked at the tent and couldn't see any stovepipes sticking out.

"What's wrong with the stove?" I asked.

"Nothin'," he responded.

"How come you're not using it, then?"

"There isn't one. I've been through every box and if there's a stove here, I sure can't find it anywhere."

"You know what you're looking for, don't you?" I asked, rather sarcastically.

"Yeah," he snarled. "I know what a stove looks like. And I'm telling you there is no stove."

"Shorty. It's probably in that miserable little mother's pack," I said, and dug out the groceries for the night's menu. "It's okay, I'll cook over the open fire. You know, it's such a beautiful evening that it would be a shame to waste it cooking inside."

Supper was on when the wrangler and Shorty arrived. Shorty was obviously no longer considered trustworthy, as he was snugged up tight on a lead rope.

"You better sit and eat while it's hot," I told the wrangler. "Then after supper you can look to the horses and finish unpacking. We couldn't find the stove, so it must be in Shorty's pack."

After supper, I collected a bunch of nice, fully-needled spruce boughs to make myself a bed.

"How come you're doing that?" asked my partner, as I began cutting and packing the spruce limbs.

"I like to be comfortable when I sleep," I replied. "Have you ever slept on a spruce-bough bed?"

"Naw. Not me. I like to sleep on the ground when I'm out in the bush. I like the feel of the earth beneath me," he said, looking down his nose at my creation. "It makes me feel more like I'm roughing it."

"To each his own, my friend," I replied. "But I've slept on both, and I can assure you I prefer to be comfortable whether I'm roughing it or not. Why don't you cut some kindling for the fire tomorrow morning?"

"Don't you worry about the morning fire. I'll take care of it," he said, lounging against a spruce tree, enjoying the beauty of the evening.

"Speaking of fire, where's our stove?" I asked the wrangler. "I expected to see it up by now."

"There's no stove," he replied. "I've gone through everything and I can't find one."

"You're kidding me, right?"

"No, I'm serious," he replied. "There's no stove."

"I told you there was no stove," my partner chimed in.

"Well, that's a pile of bull. Look, I contracted for a complete pack trip, and that includes a stove. Now, I bloody well want a stove!" I shouted at the poor wrangler, who couldn't get a stove out here for any money.

"Slow down," said my partner, the expert horseman. "We'll cook over an open fire. You're getting soft. First you want a fluffy bed and now you want a stove. You want we should get you a bubble bath, and maybe a girl too?" They both laughed.

"I'm going for a walk," I announced and started down the trail towards the meadows and Rock Creek. The Starlight Range and Arcturus Peak were right ahead of me as I walked down the trail. It was a beautiful evening, and at that point, I figured that hanging around camp with those two wasn't going to enhance my trip of a lifetime.

I returned to the camp just as the sun was sinking. The mountaintops were still bright with the last rays, and peace and tranquillity lay all around us. A pot of fresh coffee was on the open fire. Now, this is what a trip of a lifetime is all about, I thought, as we sat around the fire swapping stories of past adventures.

Daylight turned to dusk and finally night. A big old harvest moon hung in the sky. The mountains and valley took on an eerie glow under the light of the moon and the million stars that twinkled overhead. Yes, it was bright on that cloudless, peaceful night when we finally turned in. Snuggling down on my comfortable spruce-bough bed, I was able to make out the shadows of the trees on the roof of the tent.

Except for the expert horseman, Shorty, no stove, and the fact that I had had to unpack the horses myself, it had been a beautiful day. I had to admit that overall it was a great start. I smiled to myself as I drifted off.

Sometime in the middle of the night I was awakened. "Bob," I thought I heard a distant voice calling. Was I imagining it, or was someone actually calling my name? I opened my eyes and looked around. There was no longer any light inside the tent. The night was pitch-black. I looked straight up, but could not see anything. Not even a shadow. Somewhere in the distance I heard the tinkling of a horse bell.

"Bob." There it was again. This time, I knew I heard it. Someone calling my name. This time it was much closer.

"What?" I answered, half asleep.

"Are you cold?" asked a quavering voice. It was my partner. The guy who liked to rough it.

"Me? Cold? No way." I chuckled. "I'm nice 'n warm 'n toasty. How are you doing, down there on the ground?"

"I don't know what's wrong, but . . . well, I feel cold and I'm wet. I think I'm freezin' to death," he moaned.

"Did you pee yourself?" I asked and couldn't help but laugh at the little joke.

"It's not funny!" he wailed, and I could hear his teeth chatter. "I . . . I'm cold an' . . . an' wet an' . . . I . . . I can't sleep."

By now, I was wide awake and my eyes were becoming accustomed to the dark. It was a good thing, because everything was so black that I couldn't see a thing. Even the shadows of the trees on the tent had disappeared. I stuck one hand out from my sleeping bag and touched the ground. The soil and the duff on the ground were bone dry.

"It's just your imagination. This campground is good and dry. Go back to sleep."

And with that I snuggled down in my sleeping bag on my bed of spruce boughs and drifted off again.

There was no sign of light a short time later when my partner stumbled out of bed.

"I've got to light a fire," he said, his teeth chattering like a handful of dice. "I . . . I'm about f-f-freezin' to d-d-death and I . . . I . . . I'm s-s-soakin' w-w-wet."

My partner fell around on the inside of the tent as he looked for the matches. He knocked over the boxes with the groceries. Cans rattled and flew in all directions. He stepped on both me and the wrangler half a dozen times. He cursed and swore a blue streak as he bumped into everything and everybody in the total darkness. We were all wide awake long before he finally found a match.

"How about you?" I asked the wrangler. "Are you cold and wet too?"

"Just tired," he muttered.

"Maybe you just feel cold and wet when you're roughing it," I joked, and the wrangler and I both laughed.

49

"Something's wrong with the tent. I keep hitting my head," mumbled my partner, as he knocked over a stack of pots in the darkness.

I raised up on my elbow facing the noise, and as I did, something cold and damp hit me square in the face. Oh no, I thought to myself.

Finally, my partner found a match and lit it. I was lying on my back looking skyward. In the dim light cast by the flickering match I could see that the tent was now only inches from my head, whereas it had been up better than four feet the night before.

"Ooh-ooh, this doesn't look good," I said. "I think maybe it's snowed during the night, and by the look of the roof of the tent we had a good dump too." The snow lay heavy on the tent, and the roof was sagging under the weight. There was barely enough room to crawl around inside; there was certainly no room to stand up.

No wonder the expert horseman had been having trouble moving around. After he got the Coleman lantern lit, he dug out some dry clothes and put them on.

"Here, you guys, look at this," he whined, holding up his nightclothes. "You can wring the water out of them." There was no doubt about it, my partner was one cold and wet dude all right.

"Well, I don't know how you've got so wet," I replied. "Everything else in here is nice and dry."

"I have no idea either," he moaned. "All I know is I'm soaked and damn near froze to death."

I leaned over and touched his sleeping bag. It was about as cold and wet as my partner. Then I spotted the problem. When my partner decided to rough it, he chose a spot right next to one of the walls. Sometime during the night, he stuck a corner of his sleeping bag under the wall of the tent, into the great outdoors.

"Well, it's no wonder you're wet," I chuckled. "But I have to hand it to you, old man, when you decide to rough it, you really go all out. Look where the bottom of your sleeping bag is — it's outside, drinking up all the moisture from the fresh snow."

Since he was already up, my partner decided he might just as well start breakfast. First he had to light a fire. Out in the snow and the cold, I could hear him cussing a blue streak as he struggled to make a fire. All the nice dry wood that had been lying around the firepit or stacked under a tree last night was still there, but now it was in the same condition as he was, cold and very wet.

"I tell you, experience is a great teacher," I mused. Both the wrangler and I had a good chuckle over that.

My partner was a persistent devil and eventually, with persistence and the help of almost every piece of paper in the tent, he got a fire going.

"If it's all the same to you, I'm just going to lie here in the comfort of my spruce-bough bed until breakfast is ready," I called to the morning chef.

I love the smell of frying bacon anytime, but the smell of frying bacon drifting through a campsite way back in the mountains has a very special appeal. Rarely did I have the opportunity to lie in bed and enjoy the smell of bacon frying over an open campfire. Bacon and eggs! What a way to start a day, I thought as I lay back in the dry warmth and comfort of my sleeping bag. I savoured the moment.

"Breakfast will be ready in a minute!" yelled my partner from his snow-covered kitchen.

"Good," I called back, "I'm hungry enough to eat a horse." I crawled out of the sack. But I had to step back, for the wrangler had been on the trail before. He sprang out of bed already dressed, and bolted for the fire. I dressed and went outside to wash up. I stopped at the campfire, where my partner huddled over the flames like a frozen turd. The wrangler was leaning against a tree. He seemed to have lost some of his enthusiasm for breakfast. I took a look at the pan nestled in the burning wood. There were little flames dancing around the bacon. Big flames on the outside of the pan, little flames on the inside of the pan. I took a second look. Of course, I was wrong. Those weren't little flames at all; they, too, were big flames. It was hard to believe, but there was as much fire inside the pan as there was outside the pan.

"What's this?" I asked very sarcastically, as I watched our carefully measured first morning's breakfast burn. "Are you doing bacon *flambé* for breakfast?"

"Just look after yourself," he snarled, "and be ready to eat when I serve it."

It appeared to me that the bacon was maybe just a tad overdone. What the heck, I thought, I like crisp bacon, and if someone else is cooking, I could live with it a little crispier than crisp. Anyway, you don't argue with a cold, wet, snarly cook—especially when he happens to be holding a flaming pan of bacon.

"It's ready, come and get it while it's hot!" yodelled my partner into the brisk mountain morning. Into the tent he came, carrying three plates, and set them on a pack box. It was the happiest he'd been all morning. He pulled up a second pack box and grabbed a plate. He dug into the contents, shovelling them in as if it were his last meal. Now, I've seen folks who enjoyed cooking and enjoyed eating, but I never saw anybody enjoy his own cooking as much as my partner did.

"Mmmm," he groaned. Then he shovelled in another mouthful. "Oh man, is this ever good," he purred to himself and in went another heaping forkful. "Have you guys ever tasted anything so good?" he asked, and his eyes rolled towards the heavens.

I looked over at the wrangler, who had picked up his plate. He wasn't nearly as thrilled with his offering. He was sitting there, holding the plate and staring at the contents as if he couldn't believe what he was seeing.

I looked at my plate and then back at the wrangler. He still hadn't touched his plate; his eyes were riveted to it in disbelief. Unlike my partner, he was speechless.

I left my cohorts to their own world of disbelief and turned my attention to my plate. I sort of figured that if I could identify it, I could eat it. But, for the life of me, there was nothing in the charred substance that was recognizable. My plate looked suspiciously as if the cook had scooped up some of last night's ashes and coals, and served them. I touched them with my hand. No, they were still warm; it was definitely this morning's burnings. I walked over to my partner, certain that he had kept the bacon and eggs for himself, but I was wrong. There he was, shovelling the last of the charred remains from his plate into his mouth.

"Mmmm," he cooed. "Now that's what I call a breakfast," he gurgled as the last of the ashes disappeared. There was no doubt, my partner was enjoying his breakfast.

"To what great honour do I owe this burnt offering?" I asked the cook. As the trip of a lifetime progressed, I was certainly getting a better appreciation for his expertise. Now I certainly knew what he had meant when he said, "I cook a mean spread of bacon and eggs over an open fire."

"What's wrong with them?" he snarled defensively.

"Well," I began. I didn't want to offend him any more than he already was. "I prefer to have my bacon just a teensy bit less crispy, and the eggs with the yolks just a mite softer then these. Sort of, well, you know, just a little on the runny side."

"On the trail ya eat what's cooked," he snapped. "Anyway, scrambled eggs don't have runny yolks."

"Ah, yes," I said taking another look at the plate. "Scrambled eggs it is! That explains it, then. I'm truly sorry. I really should have known that." I looked down at the plate and noticed a slight wisp of smoke curl up from what may or may not have been the scrambled eggs. "Thanks for clearing that up for me. It was rather foolish of me to think they were fried."

I shot another glance at the wrangler. He had the same serving as I, and he was still trying to stare down the contents of his plate.

"It's bacon, fried crisp, and scrambled eggs," I informed him.

"Oh," he mumbled, and looked at me as if I had lost my mind.

I couldn't put my finger on it, but for some reason I had lost my appetite. Bacon and eggs over an open campfire had suddenly lost their appeal.

"I guess I'm not as hungry as I thought," I said to the cook, "but seeing as how you enjoyed yours so much, you can have mine." I put the plate down in front of him and walked out of the tent, into the forest, into the clouds. I needed some fresh air.

"I don't think I'm hungry either," I heard the wrangler say, and he followed me outside, into the early morning. "If I'm going to keep doing this, I think I better learn how to cook," the wrangler mumbled as he walked by.

"I know the feeling," I chuckled. "Isn't it funny how you sort of take cooking for granted until you run into an expert?"

It had snowed a good foot overnight and it was still coming down. The clouds hung so low that you could actually watch them slowly move along the ground through the trees. The trail, only a few feet away, was often impossible to see. It was a good day to lie around camp and wait for the weather to break.

"Tomorrow will be a better day," I informed the wrangler. "This stuff never lasts more than a day." I crossed my fingers and looked skyward at that statement. This could be a very long trip of a lifetime.

My partner spent most of the day trying to dry his

clothes and his sleeping bag. Not an easy feat over an open fire with heavy snow falling. He worked like a busy little beaver throughout the day and most of the night keeping that fire going.

The next morning the weather was no better. It was still snowing. Neither my partner's disposition nor his cooking had improved, and his sleeping bag was still pretty wet. He was also gaining a healthy appreciation for sleeping on hard, rocky ground. It appeared that this roughing it was considerably rougher than he had bargained on.

For the second straight day, I passed on breakfast, the snow fell, the clouds hugged the mountains, and my partner did his level best to dry out. The trip of a lifetime was starting to lose some of its appeal. The happiest person in camp was the wrangler. He sat around and entertained us with outfitter-type stories. They were mostly about dudes and horses in the mountains. Dudes who didn't know a bloody thing about camping and trail riding. Dudes who would have made his life easier if they had stayed away. This trip had to be the easiest job the wrangler ever had, I thought, watching him drink tea by the gallon and eat everything he got his hands on. Everything, that is, except breakfast.

By noon, I had had enough; it was time to make a move. "Saddle up my pony," I said to the outfitter. "I'm going to ride on down the trail towards mile 58 and the Summit Cabin. I might even go as far as the Sulphur River. Hopefully, this cloud is just hanging over this mountain and it'll be clear to the west of us."

The wrangler looked at me as if I were crazy. "You're not goin' out alone . . . in this pea soup?" he exclaimed, realizing that his gravy train was about to end.

"You got that right," I replied, "you're going with me." I smiled at him as the message he was dreading sank in. "How does that sound?" I could tell by his face that it hadn't sounded good, but he slowly pulled himself up and started for the flap on the tent.

"I'm going, too," chirped my partner. "Saddle up Thunder for me."

"I think somebody should stay at the camp," I suggested.

"Not me," said my partner. "I'm ready to ride."

"I'll stay," said the wrangler hopefully.

"Fat chance of that! Anyway, you're the guy that's supposed to know this country." I smiled at the wrangler. "You go, I'll stay here and keep the fire going. I'll have a nice hot supper ready when you get back."

"Hey, that's good. If you're not going, can I borrow your rain gear?" my partner asked, as he grabbed my oilskin jacket.

"What's wrong with yours?" I asked.

"It's not that good. It leaks a lot, and I don't want to get any wetter then I already am," he whined.

"I suppose so," I replied reluctantly. "Just make sure you bring it back in one piece."

I stood at the tent and watched the two of them disappear into the cloud. The last thing I saw as they turned onto the trail was the bright yellow of my oilskin slicker. The last thing I heard was my partner's voice:

"Whoa horsey, whoa now," he cooed as he renewed his acquaintance with the horse.

"Whoa horsey, whoa." I heard the familiar sound that announced the return of the two at suppertime, and it was just in time, for I had a big pot of stew cooking. Into the camp they rode, the wrangler first and Thunder following close behind. Thunder was being led back to camp. My partner was sitting in the saddle all hunched over. Once more, he looked like a frozen turd as he was led into the campsite. I noticed immediately that something was missing. The bright yellow colour of my slicker was noticeable by its absence. My partner was not wearing my rain gear. They dismounted, cold and shivering. Once again, my partner's teeth sounded like the rattling of dice. Once again, my partner was very wet. They made straight for the fire and the pot of stew; the horses could wait. The news, they said, was not good, not good at all, as they huddled close to the flames and gulped heaping spoonfuls of hot stew.

"Why didn't you keep the rain gear on?" I asked.

"I did," he replied, shovelling in another spoonful of stew. "I did right up until the time I lost it."

"What do you mean you lost it?" I asked. "Tell me, how can you lose a coat . . . a coat that you're wearing?" My partner was starting to wear just a little thin.

"It wasn't my fault," he snapped back. "It was Thunder's fault. You see, Thunder decided to take the lead. You know, like he did coming in here. Well, he took the lead for a while, and then he took the wrong trail. Somehow, we got into a stand of heavy spruce, and the jacket got snagged on something. I tried to stop him, but he just kept on a-walking. It was either me or that jacket, Bob. I thought I was gonna be pulled right off that horse. I had to shed it. Honest, I had to shed it, or else Thunder would've walked right out from under me. That Thunder's got a mind of his own, you know," he declared, glaring at me.

"That's it!" I snapped. "Come hell or high water, I'm moving tomorrow," I told the wrangler.

"Even if it's like this?" asked the wrangler.

"Especially if it's like this," I replied.

"Where we goin' to?" he asked.

"I have no idea," I replied. "Somewhere, anywhere, away from here. You pick a spot."

Next morning I woke early. I was ready to hit the trail. Not being the cook, I was generally the last one out of bed in the morning, but not today. This was moving day. Time to get up and packed and on the trail. This day, in spite of the snow and cloud, I was a man with a mission. "Let's roll!" I bellowed. "We're breakin' camp."

The wrangler left to gather the horses. Breakfast was cooking over an open fire. I was busy packing boxes. The weather was doing its best to dampen our spirits, but moving day provided the incentive I needed. There was a new feeling of purpose in the camp. Once more I passed on breakfast. I marvelled at my partner's constitution, and how he seemed to thoroughly enjoy eating ashes, albeit warm, fresh-cooked ashes.

Breakfast was long since past, and the sun should have been high in the sky when the wrangler finally returned, without the horses. "I can't find the horses," he stated. "They're gone."

"What do you mean, they're gone?" we asked in unison.

"They're gone. I usually put the bell and hobbles on my saddle horse, but I guess I forgot last night. Anyway, they're all gone. I think they headed into the park. I'll chase them down after I eat."

My spirits were starting to take a bit of a kicking as we waited for the wrangler to return with the horses. By dusk, when he hadn't returned, our spirits were broken. Reluctantly, we unpacked, preparing to spend another night. Once more, supper was on the fire when we heard the sound of horses coming up the trail.
"Tomorrow we move," I growled at the wrangler. "And them horses had better be here when we get up in the morning."

"You decided where you want to go tomorrow?" he asked. "I didn't find any better weather anywhere I walked today."

"Rock Lake," I said without hesitation. "Rock Lake. I'm going home. You two can do what you want, but me, I've had enough. I'm going home."

Next morning, the horses were back in camp before I got out of bed. The weather had taken a turn for the worse; rain was now mixed with the snow, and the clouds were still hanging low to the ground. We packed the horses and started back through Eagles Nest Pass.

Our pack train walked slowly down the trail in the rain and snow. The trail wound down along the mountainside and crossed a small stream. Here we emerged from the clouds, for the first time since we had arrived. At least while we crossed this short valley, in the rain I could see the colours of the rocks, the grass, and the trees. Once again, I was bringing up the rear. The pack train was strung out ahead of me.

I looked at the wrangler leading the pack string, at Shorty on the end of a very short lead rope, and at my partner braving the weather in his slicker suit, sitting astride Thunder who was pushing his way into the string of pack horses. As they started up the slope on the other side of the creek, I watched my trip of a lifetime slowly walk into the clouds..

I sat astride my horse, hunched over in my saddle. I was without my rain gear, my clothes were soaking wet, and the water was running down my back into the crack of my ass. I was cold, wet, and miserable. I cursed my memories of the trip of a lifetime.

I should have listened to my mother.

THE MEXICAN HOT DOG

"Can you smell that?" asked my buddy, lifting his nose to the wind. His nostrils flared as he sucked in a huge breath.

"I sure can," I replied, and I too took a deep breath. "Man, but I love the smell of the sea. I really can't get enough of it." The setting was the Mexican Riviera, and my buddy and I were returning from the marketplace, just the two of us. We were walking on the boardwalk along the ocean, and the smell of the salt water from the Pacific was heavy in the afternoon air.

"Not the water, you dummy," scolded my buddy. "Can't you smell that?" He lifted his nose to the wind again and drew in another lungful. "Now that's what I call a beautiful aroma. An aroma to die for."

I lifted my nose and tested the wind again. Sure enough, it was there. How had I missed it the first time? I thought to myself. The aroma my buddy had detected cut through the smell of the salt water. And what an aroma it was, the smell of frying bacon, sizzling on the grill, and the mouth-watering smell of frying onions. It was a tempting, tantalizing aroma that invaded my nostrils and teased my tastebuds in the late afternoon. You know, Bob old boy, I thought to myself, a little snack before supper might just be in order here.

It didn't take us long to ferret out the source of these delicious smells. As we arrived at the street corner, the aroma grew stronger and, suddenly, there they were, right before our very eyes. Hot dogs. About a dozen of them, sizzling on a grill. But these were not just ordinary hot dogs—these babies were wrapped with bacon. They sizzled, sputtered, and spit, turning a beautiful brown as they cooked. Next to the hot dogs, on the side of the grill, was a pile of chopped onion. Fried chopped onion. The bacon, the onion, and the hot dog, they were all done to perfection.

"C'mon," said my buddy. "I always have room for a hot dog. My treat."

"I don't know," I replied. I too had room for a hot dog, but there was a terrible argument going on in my body. My brain was screaming at me, "NO! NO! DON'T DO IT, YOU FOOL!" However, my tastebuds were saying something different: "EAT! EAT! EAT!" they yelled, for they were already tasting the dogs, dogs that I had to admit smelled heavenly.

"I don't know," I said cautiously. "Hot dogs in Mexico are one thing, but from a street vendor? Man, you know that sounds to me like a blueprint for disaster."

"*Sí amigo,*" the vendor interjected hurriedly. "They are very good. They are Mexican hot dogs. I made them myself."

"Yeah, that's sort of what I'm afraid of," I replied.

"C'mon," my buddy urged. "Take a good whiff of that. Now that's an aroma to die for. Isn't that the best hot dog you've ever smelled? Let's have just one. I'll buy."

"I . . . I don't think so," I responded.

"*Sí amigo,*" added the vendor. He was already smelling a sale and was digging out two hot-dog buns. "My hot dogs, they are the very best in all of Mexico!"

"I bet they are," I replied and patted him on the shoulder. That was as close as I really wanted to get to a Mexican street vendor and his hot dogs.

"You know, I just love hot dogs," my buddy said enthusiastically. He hadn't bought one, but already he could taste that dog. The look on his face reminded me of a kid at a carnival.

Now, I'm not really a big fan of the hot dog, but I had to admit, those weenies sitting on that grill looked and smelled mighty tempting. However, I had learned over the years that my cast-iron gut was not made of the best cast iron. I knew that if the wrong stuff hit the old gut, I could heave it with the best of them. I also knew that only fools bought food from street vendors in Mexico. Still, with the smell of the sizzling bacon and the onions frying alongside them, my tastebuds were watering. Yes, those weenies, they did look tempting.

"I'd love to, but . . . a hot dog . . . from a street vendor . . . in Mexico . . . I'm sorry," I said to a saddened buddy. "I think I'd feel safer with a drink of water off the street. The water will only make you sick. This stuff could kill you. I'm really sorry, but I've got to pass, man."

My buddy was dumbfounded, deflated. All the wind had been let out of his sails. He just could not believe that anyone could turn down such a delicious-smelling dog.

"If I ate that, I know I'd be playing with fire," I said. "But you're a big boy, my friend. If you want one, go for it, man. Don't let nothing but gut-wrenching fear and the thought of a good fire in the hole hold you back."

"Naw, I guess you're right," he replied dejectedly. "You're right."

My buddy was not nearly as dejected as the street vendor, who had already popped two of the bacon-covered weenies into buns and smothered them in onions. He was following us down the street, still trying to make the sale.

"*Señores . . . señores,*" he wailed as he ran alongside us. "Here, *señores*. These are for you. I make them *especial* for you. They are the best hot dogs in all of Mexico!"

That was not the end of the hot-dog caper. The little street vendors were everywhere. Wherever we went, they were there—the smell of the bacon, the onion and the weenie, teasing, tantalizing. And each vendor had the best hot dogs in all of Mexico. I know, for each one told us so.

A couple of days later, I popped into a shop to look at some Mexican cowboy boots. My buddy waited outside, so I had a quick look and left. When I came out, my buddy looked like a kid who has been caught with his hand in the cookie jar. He hadn't expected me to return so quickly, and there he was, trying to cram the last piece of a hot dog, wrapped in bacon and smothered in onions, into his mouth. He was able to jam the bun, the hot dog, and the bacon in, but the onions shot out like little missiles and splatted on the sidewalk.

"You didn't do that, did you?" I asked as I walked over and checked out the onions spewed on the cement.

"Mmmph," he replied, trying to chew and swallow at the same time. Finally the last of his ill-gotten gains slipped down, and he just looked at me with a grin on his face as wide as all get-out. "And, I'm here to tell you, mister man, it tasted even better than it smelled, too!" he crowed.

Every time I looked at him for the rest of the afternoon, he was grinning like a Cheshire cat, happy and content. Yeah, my buddy had finally gotten his wish, a Mexican hot dog.

That evening during happy hour, while the rest of the group chatted happily and slurped up margaritas, I noticed that my buddy was unusually quiet and he was not slurping. He was sipping, much more slowly than his normal pace.

"Are you okay?" I asked him.

"I'm fine," he replied. "Why?"

"Well, I don't know. You sorta look a little green around the gills," I kidded him. "Besides that, I think maybe your margarita is getting a little warm."

"I'm just coasting," he replied. "Just coasting."

Then, a strange growl was heard above the chatter. It seemed to be coming from the direction of my buddy's belly. During the growling, which seemed to last an awfully long time, my buddy's face, although he did his best to hide it, was showing tell-tale traces of discomfort. His face paled and his lips turned purple. He gritted his teeth and squinted his eyes until the growling subsided.

"What was that?" asked one of the ladies at the table.

"Sounds like a dog to me," I laughed. "A Mexican dog."

My buddy gave me a weak smile.

"You better take that puppy for a walk," I chuckled. "You don't want to let that thing out in here, or there will be an aroma to die for."

"Well, I think you better go and get it something to eat," said the lady, howling with laughter.

"I'm fine," he squeaked with a sickly grin. "I'm not hungry. I can wait."

"Well then, give it a good drink," she laughed. "Maybe you can drown it."

"I know," I piped in. "Why don't you feed it a hot dog? You know, one of those hot dogs wrapped in bacon and smothered in onions. Like the ones they make on the street."

"A Mexican hot dog! Don't you even think of doing that," interjected my buddy's wife. She hadn't said too much during the growling, but she certainly piped up and added her two cents' worth at the suggestion of a Mexican hot dog. "I think I'd sooner take my chances eating a half-cooked chicken than one of those hot dogs. Did you see how they store those things?" she asked.

"Yeah," I replied. "They've got them in little coolers."

"Little coolers, my eye," she snorted. "The ones I've seen keep them right in the street carts. I never saw any coolers, and there's certainly no refrigeration or anything like it in those carts. That food sits out there in the sun all day long. That's a great place to get a gut-wrenching case of salmonella. You eat one of those things and you'll be lucky if all you get is the screamin' meemees," she added.

"That's right," added the lady who had been the first to comment on the growling. "I'll bet you could even get Montezuma's revenge from one of those." The growling had not ceased during this little discussion.

"What d'ya say?" I asked my buddy, chuckling. "Should I whip out onto the street and get you a nice juicy Mexican hot dog, so you can feed that little growl of yours?"

My buddy wasn't laughing. He failed to see the humour. The longer we sat, the greener he looked. Somewhere during our little discussion, the growling had turned to rumbling. The rumblings, like labour pains, were coming more frequently and getting closer together by the time the third round of margaritas was ordered. It was totally out of character, but my buddy had yet to finish his first cocktail.

Then he excused himself from the table. He took a few tentative steps towards the door marked *HOMBRES*. Suddenly, there was a huge rumble. It stopped him in his tracks, but not for long. For a split second he paused and stiffened. He stood up straight like a post. The rumbling stopped and he sort of relaxed, but it was a false sense of security for he immediately stiffened again. I thought I heard the cheeks of his butt slam shut. He was no longer hesitating. Instantly, my buddy was all action. He pushed aside people, chairs, and people in chairs as he charged across the floor. My buddy was a man with a mission, and he was wasting no time as he headed for the door marked *HOMBRES*.

"How are you feeling?" I asked when, after a prolonged absence, my buddy finally returned to our table. He was as white as a sheet, and he was walking much more slowly.

"Oh Lord, I'll bet that I can hit the eye of a needle at two hundred paces right now," he moaned. His voice was almost a whisper. "I have to go back to the hotel."

"Do you think maybe one of those hot dogs would straighten you up?" I asked kiddingly. "My treat this time."

But my buddy didn't answer—he had received another message. He spun around so fast that I feared he might have given himself a severe case of whiplash. Once more he was racing towards the door marked *HOMBRES*.

For the next three days, that delicious, "best hot dog in all of Mexico" stayed with my buddy. The pained look on his face was a constant reminder that the screamin' meemees his wife had spoken of were also present. In fact, I think his Mexican hot dog had been so good that it had delivered a whole chorus of the screamin' meemees.

The next time I saw a street vendor selling Mexican hot dogs, I stopped, took a deep breath and savoured the glorious aroma — an aroma to die for.

THE RUSSIAN REDS

"Bob, how would you like to go after some reds?" asked Joan, Captain Don T.'s better half.

I had to chuckle at the offer. Joan is quite a character, and I was sure that she was pulling my leg.

"You're kidding me?" I asked in reply. "Reds?"

"No, I'm serious. The Russian is full of them."

"Right," I replied. Now I was sure that she was pulling my leg. "Except for China, Russia has more Reds than anybody."

"No, no," Joan laughed. "The Russian River. Here in Alaska. It's full of reds. Right now there's a heavy run on; it's the biggest they've had in years. If you want, we can stop there on our way to the fish camp."

"What's a red?" I asked. I'd never heard the term before, but I presumed it had something to do with fishing.

"Sockeye," she replied. "Sockeye salmon. The

Russian River is full of them right now. Everybody's getting their limit."

"Is that right?" I chuckled. "And what's the limit?"

"It's usually three, but there's so many fish that they've upped it to six." Joan was getting pretty excited just talking about it.

"Well," I replied, "fishing is one of the reasons we came up. I suppose that it would only be neighbourly to help out the Alaska boys by removing some of that overcrowding problem in the Russian."

"I'll phone Donald and have him meet us there with the equipment. Donald hates this kind of fishing. He likes it when he's in his boat, taking out charters for kings or silvers." She laughed as she dialed the phone. "But I like fishing for reds. It's a lot of fun."

"They're really in there that thick, eh?" I asked.

"Oh, yeah," she replied. "Everybody has been getting their limit for the past week. Here, just look at this." She pushed a copy of the Anchorage newspaper at me.

There on the front page was a picture of the Russian where it enters the Kenai River. The banks of both rivers were swarming with fishermen. They were standing armpit-to-armpit from one side of the frame to another. There was not an inch of space to be had on the bank or in the water. Fishermen were standing in many places waist-deep in the flowing river water.

"They must have used a shoehorn to get the last person into the lineup," I whistled. "Are you sure they're catching fish?"

"Everybody. They're all getting their limits," Joan laughed. "And Donald just hates that kind of fishing. Isn't it crazy?"

I wasn't too certain that I didn't agree with Donald (Captain Don T.). I had to admit that the masses lining the riverbanks in the picture did not really hold much appeal for me either. I was having a little difficulty trying to imagine how one would cast a line without hooking a fellow sportsman. However, the prospect of catching a salmon is a great motivator, and a picture of me holding one up for the camera was too tempting.

"Donald," Joan spoke up loud and clear, "we're going to stop at the Russian and catch some reds." I liked the way Joan handled the situation. She didn't give Captain Don T. much of an opportunity to object. It wasn't too difficult to understand, from the one side of the conversation we could hear, that Captain Don T. was not in favour of the idea. He put up a great battle, but he was no match for Joan. Being an expert in dealing with Captain Don T., it was not long before she convinced him to meet us at the Russian the following afternoon.

"Donald has some clients coming in tomorrow afternoon, so we won't be able to stay too long," Joan said as she hung up the phone.

"He is coming, though, isn't he?" I asked.

"Oh yes," she laughed. "He'll be there."

I was a little disappointed when we drove up to the banks of the Russian. The hordes of people shown on the front page of the newspaper were noticeable by their absence. That could only mean there were no reds left in the Russian. However, Captain Don T. was there to greet us, and he was not alone. He introduced Mar and me to a local named Jack, a tall, slim man who had "Outdoorsman" written all over him.

"The run's slowed down quite considerably," Jack advised us, "but I know a couple of spots that might still yield a red."

"I don't like this kind of fishing at all," Captain Don T. confided to me, but his friend Jack showed no such reluctance. Jack was just like a young colt, chomping at the bit. Jack liked this kind of fishing.

"Hurry up, let's get out there while there's still a fish in the water!" warbled Jack. "You won't catch a fish, standing around here."

"The run's over," replied Captain Don T. "I don't think it's worth taking the gear out of the truck. I doubt that you'll catch any fish now."

"There's still fish," added Jack confidently. "C'mon, let's get down to the water and catch them!"

"I don't care for this, personally," Captain Don T. mumbled. "This isn't my kind of fishing. There's too many people."

"There's hardly anybody here now," countered Jack. "Everybody got their limit this morning and left," he said, shaking his head. "You should have got here earlier. There were *clouds* of fish in the water! You couldn't even see the bottom. There were thousands of them. But I don't think we're too late; I'm sure we'll be able to find a few if we hurry up. C'mon, let's get a move on!"

Standing along the banks of the Russian fishing for

Reds was something that Captain Don T. loathed. But to his credit, loathe it or not, he was going to make sure his guests enjoyed themselves. Captain Don T. had brought along all the equipment we needed, And it was Captain Don T. who got us Canucks all rigged up with rods, reels, line, hooks, and waders.

"I said I would never do this again," he grumbled as he pulled his own waders on. The words went almost unheard, for the crew, armed with rods, reels, lines, hooks, and waders, were following Jack, running for the river. Jack, being far more enthusiastic about this venture than Captain Don T., was a whirlwind of activity. He reached the edge of the water, turned left, and charged downstream along the river-bank. He wasted precious little time. Not once did he hesitate to elbow his way in front of anyone who was fishing a likely-looking hole. Come hell or high water, Jack was going to find us a red if he had to search the entire Russian River.

"I tell you, the bottom was covered with reds this morning," Jack shouted. Then he turned around and charged past us, going upstream. We all ducked to one side, then once again fell in and trailed along behind.

"This isn't fishing," muttered Captain Don T., who had taken up a position at the back of the line.

Then, without warning, Jack suddenly made another about-face and came charging back down the path. The trailing party scattered, so as not to be trampled by the determined guide.

"I told you, this is not fishing. I hate this kind of fishing," Captain Don T. declared, once again sidestepping Jack. "It's too crowded. There's no enjoyment in this."

"Here's two!" yelled an excited Jack. He had stopped and was pointing to a spot in the stream close to the far bank.

"C'mere, Bob," he called out. "C'mere. See them?" he asked, pointing out into the swirling water.

I searched the swift-flowing water. I could see a jillion rocks. Rocks of all colours and shapes. I could see the ever-changing sheen on the surface of the water. I could see swirling current. I could even see the rocks as they appeared to dance under the swirling current. However, I couldn't see anything that looked like a fish, let alone a Russian red.

"I can't see a thing," I finally had to admit.

"Nothing!" Jack said as if he could not believe his ears. "Nothing?"

"Nothing," I replied. "Nothing but rocks and water."

"Of course you can see them," Jack replied. He sounded a little frustrated. He had worked his butt off to find a couple of reds, and here I was standing right beside him, obviously as blind as a bat. But Jack was not about to give up.

"Look," he moaned. "Look at those long, greeny-blue things. Can't you see them? They're just floating over the rocks. They're right there, man, look, can't you see them?"

I looked a little harder and concentrated as best I could, but I couldn't see much beyond the surface of the water. "Sorry, Jack," I replied, knowing how disappointing it is to go to all that trouble and to suddenly find that you have some sort of misfit with you. "I'm sure they're there, but I just can't see them."

"Of course they're there. It must be your glasses," he said, trying to find an obvious reason for my shortcoming. Jack seemed to have had enough with my inabilities and turned his attention to Mar.

"Can *you* see them, Martha?" he asked. To my great relief, she confessed that she couldn't see the reds either.

"What kind of Polaroids you got anyway?" asked a rather disgusted Jack.

"I don't have a Polaroid," I replied, wondering why Jack would pick a time like this to ask about my camera. "I got a Pentax and a video camera, why?" Now Jack was completely destroyed.

"No, no. Your eyeglasses," he sighed. "Polaroid eyeglasses. What kind of Polaroid eyeglasses do you have?"

"Oh, those kind of Polaroids?" I laughed. "I don't have any Polaroids. These are just plain glasses, they're not even sunglasses."

Jack looked at me in disbelief. "How come you haven't got Polaroids?" he asked. "I never heard of anybody fishing for reds without Polaroid glasses."

"I don't know," I responded. "It never occurred to me that I would need Polaroids on a cloudy day to fish the Russian for reds, I guess. Come to think of it, yesterday at this time I didn't even know the Russian was a river, or that a red was anything but a Communist."

"Here," Jack said, handing me his Polaroid glasses. "Try mine on, put them right over yours."

"Thanks," I replied, "but are you sure you want to do this? What are you going to use?"

"Don't worry about me," Jack replied. "C'mon, put them on."

I took his glasses and was still fitting them on top of my own when Jack called out again.

"Hey!" he shouted, looking into the water without his glasses on. "I can see them fish with the naked eye. How come you couldn't?"

I ignored the question as I peered back into the water with the aid of the Polaroid glasses. About three-quarters of the way across the stream I could make out two objects. There before me in the Russian were the two reds that Jack had been pointing to.

"You're right, Jack, I can see them!" I shouted loud enough that he would be sure to hear.

"Okay, now listen carefully," Jack instructed. "Fishing for reds is different than fishing for other fish. Reds don't hit a hook. You have to drag the fly right through their mouth. Now, the minute you feel the hook touch, you have to set it or the fish will spit it out. And remember to keep the hook moving across the water. You can't let it float. You gotta put the hook in the fish's mouth."

With one eye on the reds, I waded into the water. One thing I knew for sure, if I was going to put the hook in its mouth, I was going to have to be right on top of that fish.

"That's far enough," Jack yelled. "You get any closer

and you're gonna step on them.

"Close enough" was knee-deep, about fifteen feet from where the fish were. It didn't take a brain surgeon to realize that those odd-shaped rocks on the bottom of the river were all one shape — round, like bowling balls. Slippery, slimy bowling balls. It was going to be tough enough concentrating on all of Jack's instructions without having to worry about the rushing water and slippery rocks. I was still struggling to maintain my balance when I made my first cast. I watched the hook float harmlessly along in the fast-flowing Russian. Neither red looked at it. The fly floated past the reds and on downstream. I was congratulating myself on getting the fly to float right past the fish and still remain standing when I was rudely brought back to reality.

"No, no!" Jack yelled at me. "You gotta keep that hook moving. Put it right in their mouth."

With Jack yelling advice and the rest of our party watching, I attempted another cast. This second cast was not nearly so good as the first. I figured I was probably a little tense, what with all the pressure from Jack's instructions and everyone watching my every move. I can cast much better when I'm alone, away from prying eyes, I thought to myself.

After half a dozen fruitless casts, it was obvious that I posed little threat to the reds. My ineptness was causing Jack no end of grief. Finally, he could no longer stand the agony. He rushed into the stream, right beside me. With one nifty cast, and without the use of his Polaroids, Jack dropped the fly upstream and on the far side of the reds. The fly sank to the bottom of the stream and skimmed through the current right past the nose of the reds. The fly disappeared, and in an instant one of the reds burst from the water, then turned and dashed downstream. Jack's reel screamed wildly as the fish fled in the current. I watched in amazement. I had just witnessed a real pro at work.

"Get the other one!" yelled Jack. "Get the other one, he's still there."

I didn't need any more encouragement, now that I had seen how it was done. I was thrashing the water to a froth, trying to get the other one — or one of the other ones, as several more had moved into the hole.

Another fisherman on the far bank had been watching my performance, and he decided to try his luck in our hole as well. Jack spotted the intruder and immediately took exception to him.

"He's in our hole! Hook his line," Jack hollered at me. "Hook his line, snag it, break it! Pull the rod out of his hands! Pull him into the water! That's our hole, we were here first!"

Jack had appeared to be quite a mild-mannered person when I first met him, but that guy on the other side of the Russian, fishing in our hole, had really got his goat. I took a good look at the guy. I watched his cast, and through Jack's Polaroid glasses I saw his fly pass dangerously close to the nose of a red. He retrieved his line and cast again. Automatically, I cast my line, but to my amazement, not at the fish. What was I doing? I had cast my line at the intruder's line.

"Snag his line! Snag his line! That's our hole. Snag his line and pull him in the water!" Jack hollered again.

Suddenly, I found myself caught up in the excitement of the moment. I was actually casting my line into the water right where I saw the other line. Jack would be proud, I thought; for the first time I was actually following his instructions. I was actually trying to snag the other guy's line. Missing his line, I rapidly retrieved my line and repeated the action, not once but several times. Our lines barely missed in the swirling waters. This, I thought, was almost more exciting than trying to catch a red.

It soon became obvious that I wasn't any better at catching a line then a red. I had missed both with great regularity. Then, just as I was about to retrieve my line for another shot at the intruder, my line stopped and it became taut as the hook snagged on a rock. I gave a mighty yank to free it. Big mistake. I realized it immediately. My feet slipped as the round, slimy, bowling-ball-size rocks rolled in all directions. At that moment, all hell broke loose.

My feet had shot forward, and my butt sagged backwards. Panic set in when I realized how near I was to the rushing water, dangerously close to a good soaking. Yes, suddenly I was in danger of sitting my butt down in the frigid waters of the Russian River—but I was not going down without a fight. I was pumping my feet frantically, trying to regain my balance in the wild waters. Still clutching my rod, I was doing some kind of clumsy prehistoric dance over the swirl of the water.

The snag, the taut line, and the bent rod, I realized, were probably all that was saving me from falling over backward. Then it dawned on me that the snag was moving. It was not a rock on the bottom of the Russian. It was a Russian red. Somehow, a stupid red had swum right into my hook, and he was now heading for parts unknown. Somehow, I had inadvertently set the hook and awakened a sleeping Russian red. With my butt just above the water, I was fighting the first salmon that I had ever caught in a river. I was fighting to keep my feet under me. I was fighting to stay dry. I was having a marvellous time.

"Hang onto him! Let him run!" Jack screamed at me. "Don't get wet. It'll ruin your whole day," he added with a hearty laugh.

Through no fault of my own, I managed to stay on my feet and keep dry. "Will wonders never cease," I mumbled as I regained my balance and some semblance of dignity. Meanwhile, the Russian red was still on the line, still on the run. I battled that fish as skillfully as I could. Finally, it tired and I worked it towards the bank. Several times, as I backpedalled towards the bank, I slipped on the rocks and almost joined the fish in the icy water, but through more good luck than good grace I managed to struggle to shore.

Captain Don T., not wanting to see me lose my red, had borrowed a net from another fisherman and was waiting near the shore. Now, in all fairness to Captain Don T., he is used to netting kings — fifty, sixty, even seventy pounders — in many feet or fathoms of salt water. He is not used to netting six- to ten-pound reds in very shallow, rocky water. Adding to the challenge were the many legs of other fishermen lining the river.

As the red and I thrashed and splashed into the shallower water near shore, Captain Don T. took aim on the red. The red was coasting into the shallows, heading right for Captain Don T. and the net. When the fish arrived, Captain Don T. thrust that net into the fast-flowing water. The metal hoop bounced and twisted off the rocks. The red flipped and dodged. He bounced off the net, off the rocks, and then off the net again. In a wild dash to escape, the red slammed into a few legs. Fishermen were sidestepping and trying to avoid the fish and the line.

But Captain Don T. was hot on its tail. Once more the net was thrust into the water, and once more the red made a gallant attempt to escape. Captain Don T. was fast; somehow, he got the net partway under the red and hoisted it aloft. But the red was neither in nor out. For a moment, he was balanced on the side of the net, then the tricky little swimmer flicked its tail and sailed up and over the net. Back into the water and the rocks went the red. Back into the water and the rocks went the net. The water was shallower now, and the red was having difficulty getting swimming room. It made one last lunge for freedom. Captain Don T. made a fabulous lunge for the red. The red surrendered. Not to the net, mind you, but to Captain Don T. Down on his knees, in the rocky shallows of the Russian River, he finally wrestled the red into submission with his bare hands.

"Now, that's what I call exciting!" I exclaimed as I stood over Captain Don T.

"There's nothing exciting about this," he growled as he lifted himself out of the shallows. Icy water dripped from his sleeves, his face, and his glasses. He extended an arm with a Russian red dangling from it. I relieved him of the fish and stood proudly displaying my catch of the day.

"I think I sorta like this kind of fishin'," I replied and smiled at him.

He looked at me as if I were crazy. "Good, then you go and fish some more. I'll clean your fish for you, and then we're going to the cabin on the bluff. It's almost five, and my clients should be there around six," he mumbled as he took out his knife.

"What do I do now?" I heard Mar scream excitedly. I looked up in time to see another Russian River red knife through the water. He was heading downstream and the reel on her rod screamed.

"Keep the tip up! Keep the tip up," yelled Jack, who was standing by her side offering encouragement. "Your drag's too loose, tighten it up. Keep the tip up!"

"How do I tighten the drag?" she called out as the red passed several fishermen on its frantic dash back to the ocean.

"You've got too much line out," Jack yelled as the reel on her rod continued to scream. The line had already passed several fishermen and disappeared around a bend in the stream. That was one red that had to be near salt water.

"Reel him in or you'll lose him!" Jack yelled again.

Suddenly, it was quiet. Her reel had ceased its screaming. The rod no longer pointed in the direction of the departing fish, but was sticking skyward, straight up like a flagpole. Mar had quit talking. Jack had stopped yelling directions. The line hung limp, floating on the surface of the Russian. The red was somewhere downstream, possibly in the ocean.

"I think you need a new hook on that line,"said a very sympathetic Captain Don T.

"It's gone!" Mar said, looking totally surprised and very disappointed. "I lost my fish."

"That's it," said Captain Don T. "I don't see how anyone can enjoy this. There's too many people. We're going," he said. "My clients are probably waiting for me now."

I was back at the hole, where a couple of Russian reds were still showing themselves. The guy on the other side of the river was still fishing our hole. Once more I cast my line into the current. Once more I tried to hook his line.

"That's it," called Captain Don T. "It's five, and it's time to go."

"But we just got here," Mar protested. Mar loves to fish, and she was pleading for one more chance to hook a red.

"One more fish would be nice, all right," I chimed in, also hoping that there was one more stupid red in the Russian.

"Let's go," he persisted. "We'll go after kings tomorrow. They're predicting a record run this year."

It was a couple of dejected fishermen who reluctantly left the Russian and the reds and travelled to the Swarisky Creek and the cabin on the bluff. We arrived just after six and waited with Captain Don T. for his guests to arrive. Around midnight the two clients finally drove up to the cabin on the bluff.

"We would have been here sooner," they said, "but we stopped to fish the Russian River."

"Yeah, we were there too," I said, "but it was pretty slow. I guess we should have been there in the morning. Everyone got their limit."

"Oh, we did," laughed the new arrival. "We got our limit. There weren't many reds when we got there, but when they came, man did they come!"

"Well, there wasn't that many there around five, when we left."

"You should have stayed," he laughed. "We got there about five, and fifteen minutes later the river was full of fish."

"You mean, thick like a cloud," I mumbled.

"Like a cloud," he said, and paused to think about it. "Oh no, there were more. I swear, you could have walked across the river on their backs, there were so many!"

I went to bed.

THE CARAVAN

"If you're planning to visit Fogg Dam and Kakadu National Park, you're gonna need a 4x4. And you better plan on going to the bank before you leave — a 4x4 in Australia costs a fortune," I was advised by a friend who had just returned from Australia and a guided tour of the outback. These words were confirmed by many a travel agent that I talked to prior to making final arrangements for our long-awaited trip down under.

"What about snakes?" I asked my friend.

"Well, if you stay in the cities, you shouldn't have to worry about snakes. But in the country, especially the outback and the Northern Territory, there are certainly a lot of snakes. Ten of the world's deadliest snakes live in Australia. You should be very careful."

The literature I had confirmed this:

Travellers should be careful when hiking along the trails. Many of Australia's snakes are highly venomous. Most snakes will move away from danger and will not strike unless provoked. In Australia, however, some snakes are very aggressive and have been known to attack even if they are not threatened. To be on the safe side, hikers should wear snake-proof heavy boots, long wool socks, and long baggy pants.

Armed with all the knowledge that a traveller should have and presumably would need, Mar and I were ready to tackle the best that Australia had to offer.

On week three of our Australian adventure, we flew out of Brisbane and headed for Darwin. I did a mental check to make sure that we had everything: We had booked and paid for a 4x4 caravan. We had our heavy walking boots. We had our long wool stockings. We had our long-legged trousers. Yes, we had all that preventive snake stuff on. We were ready for the snakes. We were ready for the outback. The Boeing 737 touched down at the Darwin airport, and Mar and I, prepared for whatever the outback had to offer, got ready to deplane.

We were immediately hit by a blast of hot, humid air that just about took my breath away. I looked around and discovered that Mar and I seemed to be the only two people on the tarmac who were sweating like a couple of hogs. Coincidentally, we were also the only people in the airport and, as we found out later, in the entire Northern Territory who were properly clad, ready to meet the outback and the snake face to face. Sweating like a hog was a small price to pay for one's safety. As I walked across the tarmac I silently thanked the gods for sending a strong breeze.

I had not gone far when I had to stop and adjust my load. Mar does not believe those little signs that say only one carry-on bag per person. Once again, Pack Mule Bob struggled from a plane.

The air conditioning was on in the airport (at least I think it was on), but I was sweltering in my snake-proof clothing as I retrieved the checked luggage. Sweat poured from my brow as we proceeded to the rent-a-car counter to claim our prepaid 4x4 caravan—our home for the next seven days.

"I'm sorry," replied the very friendly receptionist. That was the one thing we found we could count on in Australia, friendliness. The Australians have to be the most friendly people in the world. "But we only handle cars at the airport. You'll have to go into Darwin to pick up your caravan."

"You're kidding me," was the most intelligent thing I could think of.

"I wish I was," she replied, smiling sympathetically, "but I'm not."

"How do we get into town?" I asked.

"If you go through that door," she said, still smiling, and pointed the way to the street, "you can catch a cab right outside."

"I don't believe this," I muttered. Mar was standing by the door, guarding the mound that was our luggage. I turned back to the friendly lady. "You're sure you don't have a courtesy vehicle?" I asked her.

"Sorry," she replied. She could only shrug her shoulders and smile.

Fifteen dollars later, a very happy, friendly cab driver deposited Mar and me in front of the rent-a-car office in Darwin. The driver chatted cheerfully, and I was wringing wet with sweat as I watched him unload our bags right beside the front door. Mar went inside to check on the status of our caravan. I paid the driver, who gave me a cheery "G'day, mate!"

Our adventure was about to begin.

"Hold the cab!" I heard Mar yell as the taxi roared away into the Australian sunset.

"Can you believe it?" Mar fumed. "This is the wrong place."

"Whoa!" I screamed at the back end of the cab.

"Whoa!" I screamed again as I raced down the street, dressed in my snake-proof heavy boots, long wool socks, and long baggy pants, waving frantically at the rapidly disappearing taxi.

"Stop!" I screamed one last useless plea, but obviously the man didn't know what "whoa" or "stop" meant.

"How do you know this is the wrong place?" I panted, out of breath and sweating profusely, when I returned to her and our baggage.

"The girl inside told me they don't rent caravans here," Mar replied.

"Well, I see a lot of caravans on the parking lot. How come they don't rent them here?"

"You have to go around the block," she replied, pointing to the back of the lot. "There's another office back there that handles the caravans."

Once again Mar drew guard duty over the bags

while I wandered around the block. There I spotted a young fellow who was slowly backing out of a caravan.

"Hi," I greeted him. "Do you work here?"

"Who . . . who are you?" he asked, after he peeled himself off the ceiling. It was obvious that he was not expecting me or anyone else.

"I'm here to pick up my caravan," I replied.

"Are you sure?" he answered, flashing me a big, although rather sickly smile. Even during a mild crisis these guys disarmed you with their friendliness.

"I'm sure," I replied. "Why?"

"Because I don't have any appointments marked in the book. Do you have an appointment?"

"No, but I've got this voucher that says I get one caravan on this date from this agency. Will that do?" I asked. "I've already paid for it."

"I don't know," he smiled and scratched his head. "I only come down here for appointments, and I don't have anything marked in the book for one-thirty." He paused for a moment, then added, "Maybe I should go check again."

We both walked back into the little office, where a desk barely showed through the stack of papers that lay strewn about. He rummaged through the papers on his desk and produced a file. Inside there were several contracts for others who were picking up caravans, and he pointed out dates and times that indicated each had an appointment attached to it. There was only one more for that date, and it was not until four o'clock, and was definitely not for one Bob Adams.

I retrieved my voucher and confirmed that the date

was correct, making a few mental notes to discuss this matter in full with my travel agent if and when I ever returned from the Northern Territory.

"Look here," I said, showing him the voucher with the date typed boldly on the front. It says here that I get one caravan on this date from this agency."

"Oh yeah, mate," he replied, still smiling and friendly. "I can see what it says all right, but I don't have anything on it and nobody made an appointment. Y'know, mate, this is my first day on the job, and the only reason I'm here is because it took me so long with the eleven-o'clock appointment. I'll tell you what I'll do, mate," he smiled and looked at the heap of paper. "Why don't I just look around in here and see if I can find something?" Then he shook his head and slowly ran his hand over the desk, rearranging the paper. "If it was here, mate, I'd have an appointment marked off in my book, but I don't have any appointments till four o'clock, and I know it's not you."

By two-thirty he had gone over the papers on his desk a dozen times or more while I sat and waited. I waited, in my snake-proof heavy boots, long wool socks, and long baggy pants, in an office that had not seen air conditioning in my lifetime. Meanwhile, Mar was out on the sidewalk in her snake-proof heavy boots, her long wool socks, and her long baggy pants. She was still riding shotgun over the baggage in front of the wrong office. She had to be boiling and broiling and sweltering in the sun and the heat.

"Tell me, mate, do you get many snakes in your office?" I asked.

"Snake! Where?" he yelled and joined his papers on the top of the desk.

"No, no," I chuckled. "I was just wondering if snakes ever came into buildings up here."

"That's not funny, mate," he scolded me, "and it's not funny when you get a snake in your building either."

"Right, mate," I apologized as he carefully checked the floor before slowly edging his way off the desk.

"I don't know, mate," said the attendant. "But I don't have any record of you."

Then, for some unknown reason, he consulted the only file cabinet in sight. He pulled open the top drawer and took out a file. Lo and behold, there it was, right at the front of the first file drawer: A voucher, in the name of one Robert J. Adams, and of all things it confirmed that I had a caravan for one week, seven days.

Slowly he returned to the desk, again checking the floor around the desk and chair before he sat down. He looked somewhat dejected. "When did you say you were going to be returning the caravan?" he asked.

"Next Saturday morning," I replied. "Our flight leaves at seven a.m., so I'd like to drop it off by six."

"I see, mate," he answered. The smile relaxed me, but only for a moment. "Yeah . . . yeah I see, I see. Yeah. Y'see, mate, you've got a couple of problems: You've only paid for the caravan until next Friday, and I don't work on Saturday or Sunday. Y'see, mate, I wouldn't be here today except I had to come in for these appointments."

"I was under the impression that I had rented the

caravan for seven days," I countered.

"That's right," he replied, continuing to smile. "Seven days, and your seven days are up on Friday."

"I don't think that's how it works," I smiled back at him. "As I understand it, I rent this thing on a Saturday and I return it on a Saturday. That's seven days. Rentals work on a twenty-four-hour clock, and my first twenty-four-hour period will end sometime tomorrow, depending on when I get away from here."

"Well, mate, that's not how it works up here," he assured me. "Each day is counted separately—Saturday is one day, Sunday is one day. By this time tomorrow you'll have had the caravan for two days."

"Okay," I sighed. "Someone will pay for this when I get home. Just tell me how much I owe you so I can get on with my holiday."

"Nothing, mate," he replied. "Because it's my first day, I'm not going to charge you anything."

"Thank you very kindly," I returned his friendly smile. "Now, what do I do about dropping this thing off next Saturday?"

"Well, mate, there's nothing open that early," he assured me, "but even if there was, you don't have an appointment."

"Can I make an appointment to drop it off?" I asked, since appointments seemed to be the key.

"Yeah, mate. That you can. When would you like to return it?"

"How about six o'clock next Saturday morning at the airport?" I replied with a big smile.

"Sure," he answered, to my surprise. "I'll meet you

at the airport at six in the morning."

His four-o'clock appointment arrived, and the paperwork on my caravan had not been completed; in fact, it had not yet been started. Somewhere out on the sidewalk, I was sure that Mar must have melted into the baggage.

Finally the moment arrived. It was nearly five o'clock and I was being led out into the lot. I was going to check out my caravan. We walked past some fairly impressive units before stopping in front of a little 4x4. Instantly I thought of *The Little Engine That Could.* My second thought was that I should quickly find some place to hide before Mar saw our home for the next seven days.

"I'll run through everything with you," the attendant told me as he unsnapped the hooks on the four corners of the box. Then he crawled inside and pushed on the roof. There was a popping of canvas as the plastic roof shot skyward and snapped into place. "There y'go, mate," he smiled out at me. "There's lotsa room in here to stand up now."

I looked inside. I would have climbed in too, while he pointed out all the interior features, but there was only enough room in there for one person to stand at a time.

"Look, mate, your extension cord is right down here in this pail," he said, lifting a corner of the seat to show me a pail hidden inside. "You plug it in right up here," he continued, pointing to an outlet near the top of the caravan."

Just then, I heard a familiar voice. It reminded me

that I should have run and hidden when I had a chance. I turned, and there was Mar. She was still dressed in her snake-proof heavy boots, her long wool socks and her long baggy pants. Her face was flushed and dripping with perspiration. Mar had obviously tired of standing in the heat and humidity, waiting for me to summon her. She had left her post and joined us.

"Where's the luggage?" I asked, trying to divert her attention.

"Tell me this isn't our caravan!" she snorted.

"This isn't our caravan," I replied.

"Yeah, mate," the attendant countered quickly. "This one's yours."

"Well, I'll tell you one thing I know for sure," she replied. Mar is not particularly fond of small tight places. "I'm not going anywhere in that thing, and I'm certainly not sleeping in it." She likes small dark places that she has to sleep in even less.

"Where's the luggage?" I asked again and still received no answer. So, while Mar and the attendant went to look at other caravans on the lot, I — clad in my snake proof heavy boots, my long wool socks and my long baggy pants — raced back to the wrong office to retrieve the bags, if they were still there.

Four trips later, I was standing at the rear of our 4x4 caravan wondering how I was going to fit everything inside. Maybe if I leave the top up . . . I was thinking when Mar and the attendant returned.

"We're going to take that caravan over there," she advised me, pointing to the largest unit on the lot.

"Okay, pet," I replied and started to lug the bags

across the lot to our newly designated caravan home.

"Where you off to, mate?" the attendant inquired.

"We want to get to Fogg Dam tonight if we can, and then travel on into Kakadu sometime tomorrow," I replied, starting to reveal our itinerary while I carried the second load of bags. "I really want to see the jumping crocs, Yellow Waters, Jim Jim Falls, and the Katherine Gorge."

"Yeah, mate, well you can't have this caravan then," he said, smiling.

"Why not?" Mar demanded. "You said it was available."

"Yeah, it is," he assured her. "But if you're going into Fogg Dam and to all them places in Kakadu, you'll need a four-wheel drive. You can't get around in Kakadu, mate, unless you got four wheels pulling you through the tough spots. The roads in the park and in the outback are almost impassible without a 4x4. Didn't anybody warn you about the roads in the outback?"

I had an instant flashback to a brochure I had picked up in Canada. The front picture showed a 4x4, plowing through axle-deep muddy water. The muddy water, red-coloured muddy water, sprayed out from the wheels, coating the grass, leaves, and trees along the roadside. Everything was the colour of ripe pumpkins.

"What else have you got with four-wheel drive, then," Mar asked. We hadn't even left the parking lot, and already Mar was not enjoying the experience, and the sweat was really rolling now.

"That's it, mate," he replied, pointing us back to the little caravan.

A very unhappy Mar reluctantly stood by while the attendant finished introducing us to the little caravan.

"This is your electrical power source," he informed us again. "You make sure you stay at a caravan park at night and plug this cord into the electric outlet and into here. Don't run the lights and the fridge on the battery overnight. If you do, you'll kill the battery, mate. You'll notice, mate, that this unit also has a heavy grill protector. That's for kangaroos. There's lots of 'roos in this country so you better be careful — they're like hitting a brick wall."

The bags were moved into and out of the back of the caravan several times before I finally found the winning combination. If they were not put in just right when the top was up, there wasn't room for anybody to get in to lower the top. Even then, the last three pieces of luggage had to be put in after the top was lowered.

"Y'see, Mate," the attendant smiled at me when at last I was ready to drive out of the yard, "you think you're ready to go, but you're not. You forgot one very important thing."

"What's that?" I asked.

"Well, mate, you didn't zip up the screens in the top. You see, mate, in the places you're going, the spray from the mud and the red dust is really bad, and if you leave those screens open when you drive, the inside will fill up with a fine red dust. You won't be able to breathe." All the while he was telling me this, he was smiling and friendly.

Mar and I pulled out of the rent-a-car parking lot. Finally, my trip to the outback, the trip I had dreamed about since I was a young boy on the stump farm, was about to come true! I flipped the switch, and the air conditioning kicked in. For the first time since we had left the plane, I started to feel comfortable. In fact, I was starting to feel downright good.

"Keep your eyes peeled for a large 'roo," I said jokingly to Mar. "We don't want to hit one of those suckers."

It was getting late in the day when I turned the caravan off the main road following a sign that said FOGG DAM. We had purchased our week's supply of groceries, and the rent-a-car attendant had assured us that there were ample places to park for the night at the dam.

"Look at this," I mentioned to Mar as we started down the last leg towards the dam. "This bloody road is paved. This is great. We're gonna get to the dam in time to set up camp before dark." I pushed the pedal to the metal, anxious to get in and settled before the sun set. The 'roo-catcher was leading the way along the straight, narrow road. The sun was sinking low in the west. The sunlight was flashing through the trees, casting long, slender shadows across the road and making it a little difficult to see as we sped along.

Suddenly the 'roo-catcher leapt into the air, and the front of the caravan immediately followed suit. In a split second the entire caravan, complete with occupants, was hurtling skyward towards the tops of the trees. There was only the sound of the motor as the sun flickered through the trees.

"What do you think you're doing?" Mar yelled as

the vehicle slammed to earth. Somewhere behind me came the distinct sound of china breaking into a million pieces.

It was a perfect four-point landing. Instantly, red dust filled the caravan. A cloud of fine, red dust billowed out from every nook and cranny and crevice in the cab. The fine red dust was everywhere. It filled my eyes, nose, and mouth. It was suffocating. I was suffocating. All around me, there was only red. I panicked, and I hit the brakes as hard as I could, but it was no good, for as soon as the caravan had hit the ground, it had once again become airborne, and brakes don't work when the wheels aren't on the ground.

I was having a devil of a time keeping the caravan between the heavily treed ditches as it bounced and lurched and screeched forward. Each time the caravan made contact with Mother Earth, more dust exploded from the hiding places in the interior of the caravan. Every landing was accompanied by more crashing and tinkling from the back. I figured the destruction of the china should be just about complete. Larger bangs and bumps indicated that I was rearranging all the suitcases, bags, and boxes that had been neatly packed in the tiny interior.

Finally, the caravan bounced to a stop. As I peered through watering eyes, through the haze, I prayed that the road had not left me and I would live to see Fogg Dam and the end of the day.

"I think maybe we hit a 'roo," I mumbled when the caravan finally came to rest.

"No!" Mar exclaimed. "Is it hurt?"

"I would suspect it's dead," I replied. "I was really flying."

My knees were still shaking as I got out and walked around the caravan to assess the damage and check out who or what I had hit.

"Well, it doesn't look like I hit a 'roo," I commented. "There's no hair on the 'roo-catcher and there's no sign of one on the road." Then I noticed the culprit, camouflaged by the rays of sunlight and shadow that streaked across the road — a speed bump. Not just any old speed bump but a huge speed bump, capable of launching unsuspecting vehicles into orbit. I figure I had taken that baby at 110 kilometres per hour and climbing.

The sun was sinking fast when we arrived at Fogg Dam. There was, however, still enough light left to see the big signs that were prominently displayed: NO CAMPING.

"I wouldn't worry about that sign," Mar said. "I'd camp right here. What are they gonna do to you?"

"I don't know," I replied, "but I do know we need electricity, and I don't see anything around here, unless we can plug into the dam."

"Hey there, you can't camp here," someone yelled. It was an old aboriginal in a beat-up old car. And he had back-up with him. At least half a dozen kids.

"Why not?" Mar asked.

"It's not safe," he smiled. "Nobody ever camps at Fogg Dam."

"Do you remember where we saw the last caravan park?" I asked Mar as I beat a hasty, although more cautious, retreat back along the road, back whence we had come. The sun was gone. There were no more long shadows over the road, and the speed bump stood out in the headlights.

We drove into the setting sun and eventually found the first campground. There, in the comfort of civilization, we would spend our first night. We were almost back to Darwin. It was one black night when we finally pulled our unit into the assigned camping stall. The caravan park was almost empty and devoid of any lights.

"If you'll hook up the electricity, I'll get supper started," Mar stated wearily as she carefully picked her way around the caravan in the dark.

"Comin' up," I replied quite happily, hauling bags and boxes off the seat and stacking them outside the caravan. For it was here, under our baggage and groceries, that the good man had showed me where to find the cord. I pulled the cord out and in the dark of night, I found the outlet right beside the caravan. Right where it was supposed to be. I plugged it in and reached up to plug it into the socket near the back of the caravan. But the plug wouldn't work, for I quickly found out that it's not easy to plug a wire into our caravan in the dark, especially when one is trying to plug a female end into a female end.

"I think I'm missing a part," I muttered. "I've got two female ends here."

"Maybe you plugged the wrong end into the post," Mar offered helpfully.

"I doubt it," I grumbled. "Both ends fit into the post.

This stupid cord has a female end on both ends."

"Well, didn't he show you where to plug it in?" Mar asked.

"Yeah, he did," I snarled. "Right here. But it don't fit! Check that pail again and see if I missed a piece of something or other."

"There's nothing else in the pail," she sang out. "Maybe you have to plug it into the inside."

"Good thought," I agreed. I moved the rest of our baggage outside onto the ground and climbed into the caravan to check out the inside.

"Does it go in there?" she asked, pointing to another outlet.

"Nope," I replied. " It don't go nowhere. I'd say it looks like we eat in the dark tonight, and I'll find the outlet in the morning when there's a little light."

"Let me try," Mar said, taking over the cord. "You set the table up."

While Mar looked to hook up our electricity, I looked for the table and chairs.

"I can't figure out how this thing works," Mar grumbled, "and I can't plug it into anything."

"That's good," I replied, "because I can't find a table or a single chair."

"You've got to be kidding," she stated. "Didn't you ask him where the table was?"

"Sorry," I replied. "I was so happy to know where to plug the electricity in and fill the tank with water, I never even thought about a table."

"Well, where'd you look?"

"Everywhere," I replied. "I've searched the entire

interior of this bloody caravan and there's no table and no chairs."

"Let me look," Mar offered and tried to push into the caravan. That was when she discovered, to her horror, that the caravan would accommodate only one person at a time. Mar evicted me and gave that interior the once-over. More red dust rose into the night air as she explored every little nook and cranny. But the table and chairs were just like the plug-in — elusive, or non-existent.

At least we were able to access the water and get the propane burner working. At great risk of running down the battery, we kept the interior lights on and quickly cooked our first supper.

"Do you want to eat out of a pot or a frying pan?" Mar asked.

"What's the matter with the dishes?" I asked.

"They're all broken," she replied. "What do you want, pot or pan?"

"Whatever," I muttered, "whatever."

Mar dined on the fridge; I spread my meal on my lap. We had decided to turn in early, and the lack of lights only confirmed that it was a good decision. Everything, including Mar and I, had to fit back into the caravan. It was only after some very carefully chosen words — careful, because this adventure had deteriorated into a potentially explosive situation — that Mar was ready to make the bed.

And the bed was another matter.

"This is a joke!" Mar snapped when she looked at the bed. It stretched right across the seating area over to the cupboards, the stove, and the fridge. It was only slightly larger than a toboggan.

"This is it," I replied.

"Well, I'm not sleeping in there. There's no room."

"We'll certainly be close," I agreed.

"Turn on the air conditioning," Mar said. "Or we're going to perish in here tonight."

"Right," I laughed. "Air conditioning coming up." I crawled into the caravan and unzipped the two little side windows.

"What's that?" Mar asked.

"That's your air conditioning," I replied. "However, it works better when the caravan is moving."

"No! You've got to be kidding," she said. "I don't believe this."

"Believe it," I replied. "No power, no air conditioning."

In the already-sweltering heat, with the temperature rising, Mar and I prepared for bed. Now, if we thought it had been crowded before, getting undressed and ready for bed was a whole new adventure. After a considerable amount of pushing, shoving, and jockeying for space, we agreed that it would be best to begin outside; then, one at a time, we would climb back in. Mar, being the smallest, was the first to shed her snake-proof heavy boots, her long wool socks, and her long baggy pants. She flung her clothing into a small area near the rear of the caravan and hastily leapt inside, just in case a snake should be lurking nearby and take advantage of her when she was most vulnerable. She re-entered our sleeping quarters and claimed her space. It was a decision that was quickly disputed, for I had nowhere to fling my clothes, and when I crawled in, there was no place to lie down.

"Move over," I asked.

"I'm over as far as I can get," she replied.

"Well, you'll have to move farther," I assured her.

"Which way?" she asked.

"Your choice," I laughed. "There's as much room on one side as the other."

Reluctantly, Mar moved towards the centre of the caravan. I carefully wedged my carcass between her and the outside wall, but there was still not quite enough room. As I slid down between a wall and a hot sticky body, something had to give. The wall didn't; Mar did. About the same time as I hit the mattress, Mar was slammed up against the cupboards, the stove, and the fridge.

"Get over, you're squishing me, you big oaf," she complained.

"I can't," I laughed. "I'm right tight up against the wall."

"Well, I'm squished up against the cupboard," she complained.

"What do you think you're doing now?" she asked as I began to squirm around.

"I'm sweating like a stuck pig," I moaned. "I'm trying to get my T-shirt and shorts off before I perish."

"Well, do it without shovin' me," she replied.

"Yeah right," I laughed.

Mar and I cuddled, very close, like two friendly, sweltering sardines in a very crowded can, in our little love bed. Lying there, ramrod straight, unable to move without disturbing the other, it was a long, hot, sleepless night. But it was the beginning of our outback adventure in Australia.

"That's the last night I'm spending in this thing," Mar grumbled as the noisy miner birds chirped up a storm when the first streaks of dawn lit up the eastern sky. "There's no air conditioning in this thing, and I have a coffee table at home that's bigger than this bed is."

"Right," I mumbled and pushed my face a little farther into the side of the caravan. It was not that I was trying to avoid her, but the heat, even at daybreak, was unbearable and sleeping, or trying to sleep, in the cramped quarters was impossible.

"So, Mar, what would you like to do today?" I asked. Day one of our holiday had been a write-off, and day two did not appear to shaping up any better.

"We're going back to the rental agency and get a different unit!" she stated emphatically. "This is ridiculous."

"Right," I replied. "That means I won't have to find the electric outlet, the table, or the chairs. Correct?"

"I don't care what you do," she replied trying to get as far away from me as she could. It was no use. There was no relief. We were jammed into the sleeping place like two peas in a pod. Contact was unavoidable. It was not a pretty sight as we departed the caravan and donned our snake-proof heavy boots, our long wool socks, and our long baggy pants to take on the day.

Now, I would be lying if I said that I was surprised

when I found the doors to the rental agency closed. Locked up tight. Not even a note on the door saying when it would be open or where we could contact the nice friendly man. The agency next door, his competition, informed us that he only opened the doors when he had an appointment. Since this was a Sunday, it was highly unlikely that he had any appointments, but they were sure that it would be all right if we stayed on his lot overnight, or until he showed up.

"Well, he's gotta live somewhere," Mar chimed in. "He must have a house, or at least a phone where we can call him."

"Sorry," replied the competition. "He just took over, and no one seems to know where he's staying."

"Well, I'm not spending another night in this little crap can," Mar stated emphatically.

"Well then, what would you like to do?" I asked.

"I don't care, but I'm not spending another night in that. I didn't sleep a wink last night. That's no fun."

"Okay," I replied. "Let's go and get a nice air-conditioned hotel room."

"Then what?" Mar asked.

"Then tomorrow, I'll bring the caravan back and we'll spend our trip to the outback in a hotel room."

"But, I thought you said we paid for this thing."

"We did," I replied, "and it's non-refundable. I guess we'll just take our licks and wait for the plane to Sydney next week."

"But we've paid," Mar repeated.

So the decision, although not a popular one, was made. We kept the caravan. Once more we raced out of

Darwin, heading for Fogg Dam. In the back, our belongings, groceries, and assorted paraphernalia rattled and banged around, the result of hurried packing on my part.

"What's all that racket?" Mar asked.

"Don't worry, I'll pack it properly when we stop," I assured her.

"By the sounds of it, there won't be anything left to pack," she grumbled.

We had barely got started on this fantastic trip, and I would venture to say that Mar was not a happy camper. She was just a little bit tired from the first memorable, miserable night on the trail. Sleeping in a moving vehicle is not foreign to us, and when we travel, she often picks up a few of the winks she missed the night before. It would be safe to say that she probably would have done so on this trip, but that confounded rattling and banging in the back of the caravan would have kept even the soundest sleeper awake.

For the second time in two days, I took the last leg of the road into Fogg Dam. The shadows on the road were coming from the other direction; nonetheless, they too did an admirable job of hiding the unmarked speed bump. Mar, although very tired, was wide awake and alert. She was pleasantly surprised that I was able to negotiate this hazard without any further damage to the contents of the caravan.

Fogg Dam was not all it was built up to be. Oh, there were birds there all right, I presume by the thousands. But for the most part they remained hidden in the heavy growth that just about covered the entire surface of the dam. An expert birder would have done far better than I, for I was unable to identify the birds by the movement of grass or lily as they flew by.

After a long, exhausting day at the dam, we left and worked our way east to Kakadu. As evening descended, we finally found camping facilities at the All Seasons Kakadu Village. We must have arrived at the wrong season. Except for the welcoming committee and one other caravan, the camp was empty. The welcoming committee, half a dozen magpie geese, followed us around the campground, honking and tooting. Overhead, torresian crows, and a black kite circled our caravan.

Finally I stopped beside the best site in camp. And a beautiful campsite it was, under a monstrous tree with long leafy branches. It was some type of exotic tree that I knew absolutely nothing about, other than that there would be shade the next day. I chose carefully, for I also remembered that I had not yet found the electrical outlet or the table and chairs. Right across the road sat the other caravan, and it was all set up. They had lights, a table, and everything.

The welcoming committee did not stand back when we got out of the caravan. Those little devils pushed forward, crowding the vehicle and pecking at our snake proof-boots, our long heavy wool socks, and our long baggy pants. The welcoming committee were looking for a handout. They proved to be a noisy, pesky lot that were not easily encouraged to leave.

Once again I set about looking for the elusive electrical outlet. I hauled everything that wasn't nailed down out of the caravan. I had suitcases, boxes, bags, cushions, and seat tops scattered all over the ground behind the caravan, but once again I was failing miserably. There was no electrical outlet to be found.

Mar, however, had other ideas. Much to my chagrin, she had walked over to the other caravan to ask for help. Man, I hate it when she does that.

I had not yet finished when Mar returned with the neighbour in tow. Now, it seems hard to believe and fortunate for me, but our neighbour was an electrical engineer from Europe, an English-speaking electrical engineer from Europe. I was saved. We were saved. Our electrical problems were solved, and I had barely began my daily search for the elusive outlet.

Both Mar and the electrical engineer had taken note of where the outlet was on his vehicle. With a look that sort of said "amateur", the helpful saviour plucked my electrical cord out of the back of our caravan. With cord in hand he strutted triumphantly around to the appropriate spot and stopped. For several seconds, he stood there and stared at the smooth surface at the rear of the caravan. It seemed that his caravan was not at all similar to ours. There was no place on that solid piece of plastic for the plug. Unfortunately, the English-speaking electrical engineer was no wiser than I when it came to plugging the cord into our caravan. He also pointed out that his caravan had a table that was attached to the tailgate. He looked around our caravan until the sun sank in the west, then sadly he shrugged his shoulders in defeat, for he couldn't find the electric outlet, the table, or a single chair either.

In the gathering darkness, we watched him walk back across the road to his well-lit caravan and his supper set out on the table that was attached to the tailgate. Our would-be saviour and his wife, both scantily dressed in shorts, T-shirts, and thongs, settled down on chairs around their table. Mar and I, still in our snake-proof heavy boots, our long wool socks, and our long baggy pants, sweltered as we toiled to set up camp before preparing the evening meal.

As darkness settled in, once more we found ourselves outside in the dark, but tonight Mother Nature had a surprise for us, a pleasant surprise: A small flock of little corellas (cockatoos) landed in the upper branches of our tree. The sound of their chirping filled the evening air. I quickly forgot about the electrical outlet and hastily scoured our baggage, still strewn about on the ground, for my binoculars. I stepped away from the mess for a better look. To my surprise and delight, more little corellas arrived. And more. And more. In minutes, the tree was covered with birds, and their pleasant chirping was now a constant, incessant, deafening, squawking. And we were being bombarded.

"What's happening?" Mar yelled at me above the chattering.

"They're crapping all over us, that's what's happening!" I yelled back. Immediately, I was scurrying around under the tree trying to get some of our belongings back into the caravan. Under the tree, however, there was more than little corella crap coming down. There were leaves, twigs, branches—big branches — and there was some kind of green fruit about the size of baseballs raining down on us. The little corellas, it appeared, had taken offence to our intrusion of their tree.

That night, in the friendly confines of our caravan, along with our crap-splattered baggage, Mar and I cooked and ate. Then we made our bed. Not wanting to bare ourselves to our neighbours, we prepared for bed inside our caravan. There was a whole lot of grunting and groaning, and a few choice words were whispered as we shed our snake-proof heavy boots, our long wool socks, and our long baggy pants. For a second night, we got very close and friendly. Sticking to each other like glue, we sweated profusely through another miserable night.

The next morning, we shed our snake-proof clothing. Enough was enough. We could not, would not tolerate another day of sweltering. Out of the suitcase came the thongs, the T-shirts, and the shorts. Into the suitcase went the heavy boots, the long wool socks, and the long baggy pants. We might just as well die from a snake-bite as from the heat. Sometime during the night, the little corellas had departed. Our campsite and our caravan now resembled a huge compost pile covered with bird poop.

It was a beautiful morning; the little corella disaster could not destroy that. After breakfast Mar and I took a leisurely stroll, fresh and cool in our summer gear, along a nature trail in the Gungarre Monsoon Rain Forest. The morning air was filled with the song of birds, and for some reason the day did not seem to be nearly as hot and stifling as the first two had. We were working our way along the edge of a small lake, looking up into the trees, trying to identify the many little birds that flitted about in the branches. The trail was covered with dried leaves, making stalking difficult, for it was like walking on corn flakes. I led the way and Mar followed. We inched our way along slowly, making as little noise as possible, trying to spot the flitting shadows.

Suddenly, the leaves ahead of me began to shuffle. Then leaves exploded in every direction. Leaves flew to the left and the right as the critter came right at me. I was frozen stiff, for I knew what was under those leaves. Too late, I remembered one of the cautions I had been given:

"When you walk on the trails in Australia, keep your head down. Watch the trail ahead of you for snakes. They love to lie in dead leaves and ambush you."

"Snake!" I yelled. At the same time, I heard the leaves behind me rustling.

"Snake!" I yelled again. A brown head slithered out of the leaves almost at my feet and came right up the trunk of a small tree — a tree that I was standing right beside. The snake coming out of the dead leaves was all brown, the colour of the leaves, and I distinctly remembered being told that a brown snake was one of the most deadly in the world.

Leaves were still being tossed about on the ground by the attacking snake when its head came level with mine. For a split second, I stared into those cold, evil eyes. Then I reached behind me and grabbed for Mar, it was time to run. But Mar wasn't there. Without her snake-proof heavy boots, her long wool socks, and her long baggy pants, she was already a good hundred yards down the trail. Mar was headed for the safety of the caravan.

The snake convinced us that we had spent enough time at the All Seasons Kakadu Village. It was time for a less challenging venue. Once more, we donned our snake-proof heavy boots, our long wool socks, and our long baggy pants, then we hit the trail. We slowly worked our way into the wilds of Kakadu National Park.

We stopped at the South Alligator River, the home of the jumping crocodiles.

"You've got to see this," I had been told. These crocodiles jump twenty feet out of the water. The guy even had pictures to prove it. This day, the crocs didn't jump, nor did they show. We continued to work our way, farther, deeper into the heart of the park. It was still early when we found ourselves at a place called Yellow Waters, a place where we did find the man-eating salt-water crocodiles of Australia. During our trip along the river to view these giant terrors, I was thankful that they couldn't jump twenty feet. About a two-foot jump would have been adequate for them to get at me.

While setting up our caravan for the night, I stumbled across the electrical outlet. It was not on the body portion of the caravan, but on the cab. How stupid of me not to have looked there in the first place.

"Maybe now we can get a decent night's sleep," Mar said.

"How do you figure that?" I asked.

"Well, we have electricity now, don't we?"

"We certainly do," I replied.

"Then turn on the air conditioning," she said.

"Right," I replied. I jumped into the cab and flicked the switch.

"It doesn't work," I informed her. "It appears that the motor has to be running."

"Let me try," she replied. But alas, Mar could not get the air conditioning to work either, and we spent another hot, sticky night very close together.

The next day, we prepared for what promised to be the roughest portion of our adventure, a trip into Jim Jim Falls. Only fools would embark on this leg of the journey without checking their supplies and equipment.

Sometime during the drive towards Jim Jim Falls, the caravan developed an annoying rattle.

"What's that?" Mar asked.

"I have no idea," I replied.

"I thought you said you packed everything away."

"I thought I had," I sighed, "but I guess I missed something."

The smell of smoke was heavy in the air when we arrived at a small store to replenish our supplies. The young lady at the gas pumps told me that the Aboriginals burned small patches of park to avoid major fires when the lightning storms arrived during the dry season. As we were talking, a caravan rolled in and hot, thirsty people bailed out and ran for the store.

From their conversation, I quickly picked up that this was a party who had just returned from the falls.

"How was it?" I called out.

"Fabulous, mate!" replied the guide. "It was fabulous. If you've never seen Jim Jim Falls, it's a must. We'll be going back in about an hour if you'd like to go. We've always got room for one more."

"Don't waste your money," grumbled the last lady to stumble out of the caravan. She looked worn and haggard, although she was only wearing thongs, shorts, and a halter, not snake-proof clothing. She appeared to be sweltering in the humid heat. Her clothes were wringing wet and her hair was plastered to her head as if she had just got out of the shower.

"Why's that?" I asked. She gave me a look, as if I were daft before responding.

"Because this is the dry season. There's not a drop of water in the falls. It's a long, hot ride to see a bunch of rocks."

"Thanks," I replied.

While I waited for Mar, I thought I would check out the latest annoying rattle. Behind the driver's seat I found the culprit. Lo and behold, there, tucked in out of sight, was the elusive table. Tonight we would dine in comfort.

Our journey took us on through the park, where the country was more open. Here, not only the ditches but the hills were covered with tall grass, and all the tall grass was the same colour as the soil.

"Watch for the bustard bird," I mentioned to Mar. The bustard bird was high on my list of birds to see in

117

the region, and Mar was an excellent spotter.

"What am I looking for?" she asked.

"A bird walking on the ground. You'll know it when you see it. There'll only be its head sticking above the grass."

The heat in this area was stifling. Finally, the search for the bustard bird gave way to the searing heat and the scorched countryside. Now, when I say scorched, I mean scorched, for we had entered one of the small aboriginal burn sites. This burn went on and on. I wouldn't want to see one of their large burn plots, for this small one went on for miles and miles. We saw nothing but the ashes of what must have been tall grass. There would be no head of a bustard bird showing above the grass here.

Finally, our journey brought us to the edge of the Katherine Gorge. On the top of the gorge, it was a balmy 43 degrees Celsius. It was even a mite hot for Mar and me in our snake-proof heavy boots, our heavy wool socks, and our long baggy pants. Slowly we moved forward, winding our way down into the depths of the Katherine Gorge. On the bottom, near the river, it was only 38 degrees and for some reason actually felt cool.

Supper on our very own table that night was another experience. As soon as we stopped and rearranged our baggage, I set up the table in its rightful place inside the caravan.

"You'll have to take it out," Mar informed me. "I can't cook with that thing taking up the whole place." So, I took the table out and leaned it against the tailgate.

When she finished cooking, Mar asked me to put the table in so that we could eat. I returned the table to its rightful place. Then we discovered that with the table in place, only one of us could get in to use it. Out came the table again. I climbed in and sat on the bench, then put the table in after me. Mar doesn't like to be in small cramped places.

"There," I said, "now we can both eat off the table." Mar climbed in at the back of the caravan, and we sat there and looked at each other. Supper was on the stove and we were at the table — but the recently-replaced dishes were still in the cupboard, and with the table in place we could not get at them. Out came the table again. After four days and half a dozen attempts, we were eating off our table. One thing about our table, the first guy in was there for the duration.

From Katherine Gorge, the hottest place I have ever been, we hit the last of the highlights on our trip: Litchfield National Park, Florence Falls, Rum Jungle, Wangi Falls, and the Good Green Paddock Caravan Park finished our trip of the outback. Our last night on the trail, at the Good Green Paddock Caravan Park, we were fortunate enough to get the last stall. This caravan park is also home to a racetrack and is a very popular place. We were fortunate indeed to even be able to get in.

"The last stall is under the mango tree, right beside the racetrack, mate," the lady informed me when we checked in.

"Do the little corellas roost in that tree?" I asked.

"Oh, we 'ave lots of birds, mate," she replied, "but they don't roost here."

For the first night since we had been on the trail, Mar and I were invited to join our fellow travellers for happy hour and a barbeque. It was also the first night that we had decided to try the local delicacies.

"What's that, mate?" one of our fellow travellers asked Mar as soon as our supper hit the grill. "What are you doing to our barbeque?" I had to admit, it didn't look the same as the steaks, chops, and hot dogs that were already there.

"It's kangaroo," Mar replied.

"Oh no!" yelled the startled man. "She's cookin' Skippy. The blokes from Canada are going to eat Skippy." This little revelation was met with howls of laughter.

"Ya better throw those boots ya was wearin' this afternoon on the fire too, mate," roared another. "They'll be done long before poor old Skippy will."

"I take it you folks don't eat kangaroo," I replied. At that point the events of the evening sort of went on hold, while the crew killed themselves laughing.

Sometime during the night, I was awakened by strange sounds. Slurping. Lip-smacking. They were definitely slurping and lip-smacking sounds, and they seemed to be all around us. Then, a loud thump. My heart stopped, and my damp hair stood on end. Something bounced and rolled around on the top of the caravan. I don't know how long I lay there, waiting for something to charge into the caravan and start slurping and lip-smacking on me. But it never happened and what seemed like hours later, I finally fell asleep.

The next morning, evidence of the culprit was far too visible. What had previously been dust and little corella crap covering the top of the caravan was now set firmly in place by juice from the mango. The outside of our caravan was a sticky, gooey mess.

"That's the first time the fruit bats have been here this year, mate," said the lady when I showed her our newly-decorated caravan. "I suppose that means the mangos are ripe."

The following morning, at six o'clock, I pulled our grungy-looking caravan up to the terminal in Darwin. Needless to say, I was really surprised when I spotted the smiling face of the young man from the rental agency.

"'Ow was your trip, mate?" he asked with a big happy smile.

"Fabulous," I replied, "just fabulous."

"Did you have any problems, mate?"

"Well, the electrical hook-up wasn't really where you said it was."

"Right, mate, sorry about that. It's around the front."

"And it took me four days to find the table, and you know there's no chairs."

"Yeah, that's right, mate," he replied and kept smiling.

"But," I said and smiled back at him, "we saw everything we wanted to see."

"Good on ya, mate!" he smiled.

"You know, mate, I put over 1600 kilometres on that little 4x4 caravan, and I never saw a 'roo," I said. I looked him straight in the eye when I spoke. "And would you believe I never drove a single wheel off the hardtop the whole time? That vehicle plowing through the mud, throwing muddy water all over the grass and trees, that's only on the travel brochures."

"Yeah, I know, mate," he replied. And he, too, looked me straight in the eye, and all the while he smiled.

"WHO IS THIS PANCHO?"

"I've found him, Bob," warbled my buddy, Dale. Man, was he excited. "I've found him!"

"Who?" I asked. I had finished brunch and was stretched out under a cabana on the beach in front of the El Pescador Hotel in Mazatlán, Mexico.

"Pancho," Dale replied happily. "Pancho. I found Pancho!"

"Hey, that's great news," I chuckled. "And who is this Pancho?"

"You don't know who Pancho is?" Dale asked. He sounded more than a little surprised. "He's a guide, Bob. That's who he is. And he's really hard to get. I had a tough time tracking him down, but I found him. I thought that you, being with Fish and Wildlife and all, that you'd know him. I can tell you, Pancho is a rare find. He's one of the best guides in Mexico, and he's right here in Mazatlán."

"That's good, and what does Pancho guide for?" I asked. "*Señoritas*, maybe?"

"Anything. Anything you want," he replied. "Anything your heart desires."

"Yeah, like what?"

"Like jaguars," Dale replied. "What do you say? Do you want to go and hunt jaguars?"

"Jaguars?" I repeated. "Where do you hunt jaguars down here?"

"Pancho said he had a couple of good places. It's somewhere south of here in the jungle. And it'll only take a week. I tell you, Bob, Pancho is a rare find down here."

"Nope," I replied. For certain things, I could be tempted to leave my comfy spot on the beach, but to go driving for hours, through the arid heat to some swampy jungle where I would have to sit and swat mosquitoes, with some crazy Mexican guide I never heard of? No way. Holidays were too short as it was, and not even a team of jaguars could drag me away from the beach for a week. Maybe I could give up a *day* if the stakes were right, but not a week.

"What else has he got that's closer?" I asked. "For, say, half a day."

"Ducks," replied Dale. My buddy Dale loved to hunt ducks. "Pancho says he's got some of the best duck hunting about an hour from here."

"No thanks," I replied. I didn't share my buddy's enthusiasm for duck hunting. "I can shoot all the nice big, fat, grain-fed ducks I want back home. I'll pass on the ducks too."

"Pancho says you can shoot twenty-five ducks a day," he said, trying to entice me.

"Tempt me with something better," I said, stretching out in the sand and closing my eyes. I was enjoying another sunny day in paradise.

"Well, Pancho says there's doves and quail," he said.

"Bingo," I replied. My eyes popped open and I sat upright. "Now you're talking. When do we leave?"

Next morning, at six o'clock, Pancho arrived on the street in front of the El Pescador Hotel. He was driving an old Suburban. Pancho had promised a guide for every hunter, but he was alone in the vehicle.

"*Buenos días, amigos,*" Pancho warbled happily as he bounced out of the vehicle to greet us. "How are you this fine morning, my friends?"

"We're ready!" came four enthusiastic responses.

"That's good, my friends. When you hunt with Pancho, everybody shoots lots," he laughed. "You won't be disappointed, my friends. Pancho is the best guide in all of Mexico."

My brother-in-law, Les, piled into the front passenger seat beside Pancho. Dale, my brother Larry, and I crawled onto the first bench seat in the back.

"Where's the guides?" Les asked as soon as the vehicle pulled away from the curb.

"Don't worry, *señor,*" replied Pancho. "Pancho promised you guides. Pancho will find you guides. You wait, my friend, you will have the best guides in all of Mexico, you will see."

"Where's the guns?" I asked. "I thought you were supplying the guns."

"*Sí, amigo*, I have guns for you, don't worry."

"Do you have any side-by-side double barrels?" I asked.

"*Sí, señor.* I have all kinds of guns. Any kind of gun you like, I got it," he laughed.

"Good, I always shoot a side-by-side. It's my favorite gun."

Slowly, very slowly, Pancho drove the Suburban through the streets of Mazatlán. I guessed that he was searching for some guides to take along. We made two stops, both at hotels, and each time we picked up more hunters. It was close to seven o'clock when he turned right onto the highway leading south of the city. We now had seven hunters, but no guides.

Pancho was in no hurry. The old Suburban crawled down the highway at the same snail's pace we had driven through the city. I had expected that we would be hanging on for dear life, flying through the city streets of Mazatlán, then roaring down the highway like Speedy Gonzales. Pancho, however, did not appear to be the typical Mexican driver we had encountered.

"How far are we going?" Les asked.

"We are going about sixty miles," Pancho answered. The Suburban continued to crawl down the highway.

"Sixty miles," Les said and looked at Pancho.

Pancho looked straight ahead, at the road.

"You gotta be kidding," Les said. Les leaned over and looked at the speedometer. His head was almost between Pancho and the steering wheel.

Pancho ignored the intrusion into his space. He kept his eyes on the road.

"Does that speedometer work?" Les asked. He looked back at Pancho, then he sat back in his seat.

"*Sí, señor,*" Pancho replied. "The speedometer works. And sometimes it works very well."

"Is it working now?" Les asked.

Pancho looked at the speedometer. Then Les leaned over and had another look at the speedometer. Then Pancho looked at Les.

"*Sí, señor.* I think it is working now," Pancho answered.

"What time do the birds fly?" Les asked.

"Eight o'clock," Pancho replied. "The birds, they fly at eight o'clock."

Silence engulfed the Suburban moving down the highway at a snail's pace. I leaned forward and took a peek over Pancho's shoulder. The speedometer was registering 20 kilometres per hour. Not very fast for someone who had to be hunting doves sixty miles from here in less than an hour, I thought.

"How do you find the birds once they're shot?" Les asked, breaking the silence.

"We use Mexican hairless retrievers, *señor,*" Pancho answered. "They are the best in all of Mexico."

"I never heard of a Mexican hairless retriever," Les replied. He turned and looked at us. We all shrugged our shoulders; we had never heard of them either. "What do they look like?"

"Oh, they are very good, *señor,* don't worry," Pancho replied very seriously. "They are very good at finding birds. Do not worry, *señor.* When you hunt with Pancho, you hunt with the best. And I use only the best.

127

You will see, *señor*. Do not worry."

The miles crawled by very slowly, and the time flew by—something the birds were going to be doing without us unless Pancho suddenly found the gas pedal. This is crazy, I thought. I was starting to have second thoughts about the best guide in all of Mexico. What was I doing out here in the middle of nowhere with some Mexican I had never heard of? It was as if we were going on a Sunday-school picnic rather than a hunting trip.

Les must have been having the same thought. "If you don't put that pedal to the floor, we're going to miss those birds," Les informed our guide.

"Do not worry, *amigo*," Pancho chuckled. "I will get you there before the birds fly."

Then it got scarier, for Pancho took his eyes off the road and seemed to lock them on the rear-view mirror. It was obvious to everyone in the vehicle that something behind us was far more interesting than anything in front of us. Pancho turned around for a good look. He looked past the passengers on the bench seat behind the driver's seat, past the passengers in the third row, and out the back window.

The passengers looked at the road. Then we all looked at Pancho, and in unison we all turned and looked out the back window. In the distance, we could see a vehicle was gaining on us. When it got close enough for a good look, I could see it was a beat-up old pickup truck. Pancho smiled. He turned around in his seat, then he reached down, and from the floorboards beside his seat he picked up a pair of gloves.

"What are those?" Les asked. Les, being in the front seat and right beside Pancho, was in the best position to ask questions, and Les had not wasted a single opportunity. He asked questions about every little detail.

"These, they are racing gloves, *señor*," replied Pancho.

"What do you need racing gloves for?" Les laughed. "We're not going fast enough to pass a donkey."

Pancho did not reply. As the Suburban continued to crawl along the highway, he slowly pulled the gloves over his hands. As each glove was pulled on, and the clasp on the wrist was snapped tight, Pancho would flex his fingers. Then he would open and close his fist a couple of times. Finally, both gloves were on. Pancho turned around to face the hunters. His eyes had a wild look in them. A smile crept across his face and he turned back to the road. It was an ominous smile, the sort that made the hair on the back of one's neck stand on end. In the mirror, I could see his eyes, the eyes of the devil, and they were focused on the road ahead.

Without any warning whatsoever, Pancho jammed the pedal to the metal. The Suburban roared and leapt forward. I couldn't believe the power that was hidden under the old hood. We were all thrown against the back of our seats.

If the inside of the vehicle had been quiet before, it seemed like a morgue now. The telephone poles that had previously looked like lone sentinels out on the desert were flying by, looking now like a picket fence. Fence posts were a blur. Nobody said a word. Even Les had stopped asking questions. He had grabbed his seat and was hanging on for dear life. Les was the fortunate one, for he had something to hang onto. The rest of us, now as quiet as Les, could just look at the back of Pancho's head, at the gloved hands hanging onto the steering wheel at ten and two o'clock. I prayed that this was not the Mexican nightmare people talked about.

I snuck a peek over Pancho's shoulder and stared at the speedometer. It read 20 kilometres per hour.

"Is your speedometer working?" I asked.

"*Sí, amigo*," Pancho laughed. "I think that now it is working."

"Are you sure?" I asked.

"*Sí, señor*, I think it is working now," he answered, but it didn't appear that he looked down to check it.

Over the crest of a hill the Suburban flew, faster than I had ever believed it would go. We were heading straight for a small bridge. Beyond the bridge was a small Mexican village. Crossing the road between the bridge and the village was a flock of several hundred white chickens.

"Whoaaa," I yelled as the Suburban hit the bridge. Into the air sailed the Suburban. Into the air sailed the bird hunters. Hands grabbed for anything that was handy. Several yards later, the Suburban plunged to the earth. About the same time, the hunters slammed back into their seats.

Pancho was still holding the wheel, and he was still focused, but on a new target.

"Look out! You're going to hit the chickens!" someone yelled.

It was too late. As the last words came out of the mouth, the Suburban tore through the flock. There were several thumps and bumps as chickens hit the grill and bounced off the undercarriage. White feathers, blood, and guts sprayed out in all directions. Whole chickens burst into the air, bouncing off the windshield, some sailing right up and over the vehicle.

Inside, we all looked at each other in disbelief, then turned around and looked out the rear window at the carnage on the roadway. The pickup truck was hot on our tail. Once more chickens, feathers, blood, and guts burst into the air. It reminded me of a giant pillow bursting.

"First blood of the day," Pancho sang out as we raced through the little village.

"Geez, Dale, where did you find this guy anyway?" I whispered.

"Honest, Bob, I heard he was the best guide in Mexico," Dale whispered back.

"We can only hope there's no people on the road in the next village," I mumbled.

"No, no, *amigo*. It is too early," Pancho laughed. "People in the villages, they drink lots of tequila last night, they are still very sleepy."

We blew through several sleepy little villages before Pancho slowed and turned off the road. Into yet another sleepy little village. The streets were empty; there was not even a dog to greet us. Pancho stopped the Suburban and shut the motor off.

"We are here, *amigos*," Pancho informed us. It was a great revelation, one that we accepted gratefully, relieved to have arrived in one piece.

I looked up and down the empty street. Surely Pancho, the most famous guide in all Mexico, was kidding. The empty streets of a sleeping village was not the setting I had envisioned for a bird hunt. There was not a single bird in the sky, on the gravel street, or on the lone telephone wire strung overhead. I looked at my watch. We still had twenty minutes before the birds flew.

"Is this where we hunt?" Les asked.

"*Uno momento, amigo,*" Pancho replied. "*Uno momento.* Be patient, my friends, we will hunt the birds in the fields."

Just then a gate opened, and one of the sleepy villagers walked out onto the street. His shirt was wide open. He yawned and did up his fly as he shuffled toward the Suburban. From farther down the street another body emerged, and he too ambled our way.

"Now we are ready," chuckled Pancho. "Everybody is here. It is time to hunt the birds."

"Hey, just a minute," said Les. "Where's the dogs? I thought you said we'd have dogs?"

"They are here, too," laughed Pancho.

We all looked out at the street. Two very sleepy Mexicans had climbed into the back of the pickup. Three more were still walking toward us.

"I don't see any dogs," Les replied. I had to admit, I didn't see any dogs either.

"There they are. Mexican hairless retrievers, dogs and guides all in one," Pancho laughed and pointed at the men in the back of the pickup. "See, just like I told you. Dogs. Guides. Retrievers."

Out at the edge of town, Pancho drove into an orchard. Through the trees we drove, until we came across a parked car and several men. Pancho stopped the Suburban beside a beat-up old car.

"Okay, *amigos*, we are here. This is where the hunters get out," Pancho sang out.

Pancho led us over to the parked car and opened the trunk. There before us lay an assortment of firearms. There were guns of all types. Guns that would have been like gold in the hands of collectors, for Pancho had the biggest collection of relics that I had ever seen. Never in my life had I seen such a collection of guns, and they had been thrown into the trunk of the car, like scrap metal, to rattle and bang around on Mexican roads.

Now I was really starting to have some misgivings about this trip and about Pancho, the best guide in all Mexico. I wondered just how safe these relics might be. Most looked as if they would blow up in the hands of anyone foolish enough to shoot them. However, another, more sobering thought was running through my mind, and before I touched one of the guns, I searched the field for signs of the *Federales*. The Mexican police.

"Are you sure this guy isn't a descendant of Pancho Villa?" I whispered to Dale as I stared into the trunk. I was certain that any collection of firearms that looked like this had to be stolen — illegal guns to be sure.

"Did these come from the Revolution?" I asked Pancho. I tried to make a joke, but my eyes kept searching the area for any sign of the *Federales*.

"That is very funny, *amigo*," Pancho laughed. Then he added, "Gentlemen, it is time, choose your weapons."

"Time for what?" I mumbled.

I did see what looked like a side-by-side double barrel. I made a grab for it, but I was too late. Before I even got my hand into the trunk, Les snatched it up. He stood there, in the early morning sun, admiring the only side-by-side double-barrel shotgun in the works.

As for the rest of the guns, I decided, it was a toss-up. Each one looked to be in worse shape than the next. I looked over several of them, checking the action and the safety. Very few worked. Firearm safety and safety mechanisms seemed to be a foreign thing in Pancho's arsenal. Finally I settled on an old, beat-up Winchester pump. I pumped the action once, twice. It worked. I checked the safety catch. It worked. I checked to see how many shells would fit in the magazine. I quit at six. I checked the barrel to make sure that someone hadn't decided to hide something in there, like mud or cement.

"Are you satisfied, *señor*?" Pancho asked when I had finally finished my inspection.

"I guess so," I replied.

"Here, then," he laughed and handed me two boxes of shells, also part of the deal. Then he called to one of the Mexican hairless retrievers.

"You go with Carlos," he said. "Carlos will take you to your station."

"Do you speak English?" I foolishly asked Carlos as we walked away from the group.

"*Sí, senor,*" he replied.

In the distance, under the mango trees, there were many people. They were not hunters like us. They were all down on their hands and knees. It looked as if they were praying. Probably praying that the *gringos* could shoot straight and spare their lives, I thought. Carlos and I were walking toward the mango trees. The ground was covered with a growth of vegetation that looked suspiciously like beans. The kneelers were picking the beans.

"What kind of beans are we walking on?" I asked.

"*Sí, señor,*" Carlos replied.

"Right." I chuckled. "So, Carlos, how long have you spoken English?"

"*Sí, señor,*" Carlos replied.

"Great," I said.

Carlos and I walked on in silence until he finally tapped me on the shoulder and pointed to a tree. He gestured for me to walk over to it and stay quiet. Carlos picked out another tree for himself and squatted down. Then, we waited.

I opened one of the boxes of shells. For a moment, I thought I had a box of crayons. Every shell in the box seemed to be a different color. I had different shades of reds, blues, greens, and yellows. I had shells that were every shade of colour under the rainbow. Then I noticed the shot size.

"How appropriate," I mumbled. It looked like the shells also came from the Revolution. On the top row of shells, I saw a blue 2, a red 4, a green 5, a blue 71/2, and a yellow 9. Then I dug into the box and found some

BBs, SSGs and some 6s. There was no doubt about it, I was loaded for anything that flew, walked, crept, crawled, or wiggled in Mexico.

Before long, I heard a whistle. I looked around to see who it was. Maybe one of the kneelers had come to join us. I looked all around but couldn't see anyone. Then I happened to glance at Carlos. He was pointing frantically at the sky. I looked up in time to see two birds flying away, well out of shotgun range. I looked back at Carlos and he was shaking his head. Carlos appeared to be just a tad disgusted with the stupid *gringo* he had drawn. Then it dawned on me that the whistle was my signal. Ha, I thought, to be forewarned is to be forearmed. Now I was ready. I sat up alert, waiting for the next whistle.

Then I heard Carlos call in a loud whisper.

"*Señor, señor,*" his whisper drifted along under the mango trees.

"What?" I called back in a loud whisper.

"*Señor,*" he called again. This time, there was an unmistakable urgency to his voice.

"What?" I replied and looked over at him. He was rapidly waving an arm skyward. I looked up just in time to see a small flock of birds winging their way to freedom. I looked back at Carlos. Carlos was one very unhappy Mexican hairless retriever. Not only did his dude not respond to the whistle, he didn't recognize an oral prompt. Poor Carlos, he had really drawn a dud.

Many a bird flew safely by before my Mexican hairless retriever and I got our signals straight. Then the shooting began. I can honestly say that Carlos was as impressed with my shooting as he was with my ability to follow his signals. I was a real conservationist as I blasted many a hole in the sky.

The kneelers were long gone when Carlos and I finally walked back to the car. They had probably fled for their lives.

Yes, the hunt was over, and we were returning to the coast, to Mazatlán, to the beach and the ocean.

On the return drive, Pancho waited for no one and wasted no time in putting the pedal to the metal. Once more, the telephone poles resembled a picket fence as Pancho sped home. The sleeping villages were no longer sleeping. People were now on the road, on the side of the road, and in the ditches. There were donkeys, carts, dogs, cows, and chickens. Pancho never acknowledged any of them. His hands, snuggled in his racing gloves, were clamped firmly on the steering wheel. Pancho was heading home and nothing was going to stop him.

I leaned forward and took a peek over his shoulder at the speedometer. It was still working—we were zipping along at 20 kilometres per hour.

"Do you take out hunters all year?" asked Les, continuing the barrage of questions he had started earlier that day. Les had once more laid claim to the front seat and, like the rest of us, was holding on for dear life.

"Oh no, *señor*," Pancho replied. "Only in the wintertime during the hunting season."

"What do you do for the rest of the year?" Les asked.

"I go back to the asylum," Pancho replied quite seriously after a long pause.

"A . . . Asylum?" asked Les as the colour drained from his face.

"*Sí, amigo,*" Pancho replied happily. "My family, they tell me that I am the only one crazy enough to take *gringos* hunting. They bring me home once a year, just for the hunting season."

Les turned and looked back at Dale. We all turned and looked at Dale as a collective thought went through our minds:

Who is this Pancho?

ROSIE'S CLAM

"They called from the lake today," Mar advised me. By the tone of her voice, I knew a new wrinkle was about to be added to our plans. I could just feel it.

"And?" I asked. There had to be more.

"They said they had a cancellation and could get us in two weeks later on the 15th. They felt that would be better. They said the ice didn't melt off the lake until late this year, and the walleye were just starting to bite. The lady said the fishing should be better if we came two weeks later."

"Hey, that's great," I replied. "Two weeks later is fine with me."

Walleye fishing at the lake was always excellent during the month of June. But our fishing trips were more than just fishing, they were luxury weekends at the lake. Short of TV, the Modern Cabins at the lodge had all the comforts of home. When you stayed in the Modern Cabins, you lived the good life.

Ah, yes, I could just picture myself living the good life. There I was, just lazing about in the boat. A lone, small, fluffy cloud drifted lazily in the blue sky like a cotton ball. The sun was shining down on a beautiful day, shirt-sleeve weather for sure. The lake was as smooth as glass. In the distance, the call of the common loon. Nearby, a pair of western grebes raced across the surface of the lake, then dove head-first into the water. Yes, it was springtime in northern Saskatchewan. It was an absolutely gorgeous day to be at the lake, to be alive, and to be fishing. And to top it off, the walleye were biting as if they hadn't fed all winter. There I was, pulling in one walleye after another. There were four-pounders, five-pounders. Then I hooked him, the granddaddy of them all, at least ten pounds of fighting walleye. I was having a magnificent battle with this behemoth of the deep.

"We'll have to share a Motel unit with Rose and Les for the first night," Mar casually tossed in this little tidbit and shattered the magic of the moment. Usually we got the Modern Cabin: one bedroom that sleeps six, or eight in a pinch. But a Motel Room—that meant cramped quarters. The good life was starting to lose its lustre.

"What do you mean, we'll have to share a Motel unit?" I sat up, the imaginary walleye suddenly stripped from my line.

"Don't worry," she snapped. "It's only for one night. They only have one Motel unit vacant for the first night.

140

We can get two rooms for the last two nights, though."

"What happened to the Modern Cabin?" I inquired. "The kind that sleeps six and has a full-sized kitchen with a table that seats about a dozen. The one with its own bathroom and shower. You know, the one we usually get."

"There's none of them available that weekend."

"What's in the Motel Room?" I asked, hoping for a miracle that I knew was not to be.

"Two beds," she chirped. "One full-sized and one three-quarters."

"What happened to the bathroom and the kitchen?"

"You know the Motel units don't have bathrooms and kitchens," Mar replied impatiently. "But the lady said we'd get a partial kitchen in one of the rooms for the last two nights." She smiled.

"What's a partial kitchen?" I inquired.

"There's a hot plate and a small fridge," Mar replied. "That's all we need. We can take the small barbecue and cook outside."

"I don't know about that," I mumbled. Reality was starting to set in. After all, this was northern Saskatchewan in the spring. "It rains a lot at the lake at this time of year, and what about the mosquitoes? Who's going to stand outside and barbecue in the rain with all the bugs?"

"You," she answered.

"Thanks for nothin'," I mumbled. "You know you're not going to be able to sleep," I warned her. "We have some pretty heavy-duty snorers in our group. Remember the time we were in Mexico and the four of

141

us slept in a little hotel room? When the lights went out, it sounded like someone struck up the brass band, and you never slept all night."

"It's okay, it's only for one night," Mar responded. "So I don't get much sleep. I'm going to fish, not to sleep. I can sleep when I get home."

"I find I can fish much better when I get a good night's sleep," I countered.

"We'll manage," she replied. "And it won't kill you for one night."

"Actually, I was thinking of you." I smiled.

Arriving at the lake on the 15th, the sky was blue and the sun was shining. I pulled up in front of the Motel units.

"There's Rose and Les," Mar shouted excitedly and pointed in the direction of the Modern units. Sure enough, there were Rose and Les standing in front of one of the Modern Cabins. One of the ones with a full bathroom, a large kitchen, and a separate bedroom. Mosquitoes swarmed around them.

"What's the matter?" I called out. "Can't we check in yet?"

"We're checked in," Rose replied, swinging at the insatiable insects. "C'mon, hurry up, these mosquitoes are eating us alive. We're waiting for you so we can go fishing. C'mon, let's go!"

"Which room are we in?" Mar asked.

"Right here," Rosie replied. "They had a cancellation, so we got this cabin right here. The same one we had last year."

"Right on," I shouted. "Now, that's more like it."

Once more, the world was unfolding exactly as it should, I thought, as visions of a nice, comfortable, modern-day fishing trip wriggled and splashed their way through my mind. Yes sir, I smiled, indoor plumbing, a full kitchen, a fridge, and a stove. Sleeps six and there's only four of us. There was no doubt about it, this is the way it was intended to be. It was going to be another great fishing trip. I rushed to get my gear securely stowed in the cabin, just in case the lodge owner should have a change of mind.

The smell of citrus candles and mosquito coils greeted us as we hauled our gear through the door.

"Well, Rosie, I see you've already waged war on the mosquito population." I laughed. Rosie was no fool, she had been here before. Rosie took her mosquito battles very seriously. She was fighting fire with fire; there was a flickering citrus candle at the door and a smouldering mosquito coil on every windowsill.

"You bet," she laughed. "C'mon, get your stuff in here and let's get out on the lake. There won't be any mosquitoes out on the water."

"Have we got a boat already?" I asked somewhat surprised. Usually we weren't able to get a boat the first night.

"Yes, we have, and we can take it whenever we want it," Les stated.

"Let's go catch enough fish for supper," Mar chimed in, anxious to wet a line.

"Well, sure," Les responded, "we can do that."

"Don't count on too many fish for supper," Rose interjected. "I haven't talked to anybody who has caught any walleye. They haven't been catching anything up here. The fish aren't biting yet."

"What do you mean, they're not biting yet?" I asked. Then I looked at Mar. "I thought you told me the person you talked to said they had started biting over a week ago."

"I think she said the jackfish were biting," Mar replied.

"Jackfish are always biting," I muttered. To our group, jackfish had always ranked pretty low on the old totem pole. We liked to consider ourselves purists. Pure walleye fishermen.

"I didn't think we came all the way up here to catch a jackfish, did we?" I grumbled.

"That doesn't matter," Mar warbled. "Jackfish, schmackfish. Who cares? I just wanna catch some fish. Let's get the boat and catch enough fish for supper."

Long before our little boat made the trip from the dock to the pickerel hole, ominous dark clouds started to gather. The sun disappeared about the same time as the first hook hit the water. In the distance, a little ripple appeared on the surface of the lake.

"That's good," I noted. "The fish always bite better in cloudy weather."

I was right. "Hey, look at this," I sang out as I lifted a fish into the boat. "On my first cast I got a walleye. Who said the walleye weren't biting?"

Then came the wind, and the clouds rolled across the heavens. The little boat bobbed around like a cork. The rains came and they beat down on the lake, the rented boat, and the fishermen. The walleye, however, wherever they were, didn't realize that this was ideal fishing weather. They refused to co-operate. After that first fish, they quit biting. The jackfish, however, were a different story: they knew this was ideal fishing weather. To Mar's delight, they kept biting, hitting everything we threw into the lake. To Mar's dismay, we kept throwing them back.

"Let's keep a couple of the jacks," Mar said. As the winds increased.

"Who's going to clean them?" I asked.

"You are," she stated. "That's your job."

"Well, let's not," I replied. If there's one thing I hate worse than eating jacks, it's having to clean them. Jackfish are full of Y-shaped stickers. Bones, bones, bones. Man, but I disliked jackfish.

"Keep that one," Mar advised Les as he took a small jack off Rosie's line. "That's just a nice size for eating."

"You don't want to keep that little slimer," I declared in disgust. "Throw it back, Les," I urged.

SHPLUNK.

Yuck, I thought, do jackfish ever make a terrible sound when their slimy bodies land in a fish box. Two jackfish later, our crew could no longer take the rain. Like drowned rats, we returned to the lodge. The rain had subsided to a drizzle as we went ashore, but the mosquitoes had grown in number. Les gathered up an armful of fishing gear. He and the girls and half the mosquito population raced for the cabin. I made a clean snatch of the fish box. I and the other half of the mosquito population ran for the fish-cleaning station. Lifting the lid off the fish box and looking inside, it struck me that jackfish don't really need any water to swim in. The three jacks and my poor little walleye seemed to be swimming in the slime the jackfish had generated.

"What a disgusting sight," I muttered as I reached in and rescued the walleye. Best to put him out of his misery first, I thought as I sliced off the fillets and removed the cheeks. Then I grabbed a slimer. I scraped as much slime as I could get off the first jack, but it's impossible to get it all, and the ruddy thing was slipping and sliding all over the filleting table.

"This thing is making slime as fast as I can scrape it off," I grumbled to the fellow who had joined me. He was standing there in his own swarm of mosquitoes.

"I must have been weak in the head to be talked into keeping these bloody things, let alone fillet them."

"I like jacks," he informed me.

"Oh. Right. I'm sorry. What part of Saskatchewan are you from, anyway?" I asked.

"Saskatoon," he replied, looking quite surprised. "How did you know I was from Saskatchewan?"

"Just a lucky guess," I mumbled, and cursed as I carved the bones from the first fillet.

"Bones, bones, bones." I grumbled.

The next day was more of the same. It rained most of the day; lucky for us there were a couple of breaks. The clouds would part and the sun would come out. Like kids with a new toy, we would race the mosquitoes to the boat and head for the mosquito-free bay where it was reported someone had caught a walleye early in the morning. In the bay, surrounded by other boats, with fishermen who were also trying to catch the elusive walleye, we would drop anchor. There on the fairly smooth surface, we drowned worms, frogs, and leeches (if that's possible). We tossed minnows, flatfish, and all sorts of hardware. Once again, the walleye failed to recognize the great fishing weather and they refused to bite. But the jackfish were a different story. Then the wind would blow and the rains would follow. In spite of our rain gear, we'd all get wet. We'd fish until we were waterlogged, then Les would start the motor and head for home. What a great weekend this was turning out to be.

Back at the lodge, there was a hot shower, dry clothes, munchies, toddies, and mosquitoes. We'd sit around, telling jokes, playing cards (the best part of fishing for jackfish), and waiting for the next break in the clouds. And we would swat mosquitoes. Those stupid mosquitoes didn't understand that the citrus candle and the mosquito coil were supposed to get rid of them. Yes, out on the water, the jackfish were biting like crazy, and back on land the mosquitoes were chewing us up.

"How should we do the jackfish tonight?" Rosie asked.

"Let's not," I countered. "Let's have some of that great clam chowder you make instead." I'm here to tell you that Rosie makes one mean clam chowder.

"Okay, sure," Rosie smiled. "I'll make the clam chowder if someone brought some clams."

"I did," I sang out. "Never go on a fishing trip with Rosie unless you've got a can of clams, I always say.

You never know when they might come in handy." I went to the grub box and produced a large can of baby clams and proudly set them on the table in front of Rosie. "There you go, kiddo. Ask and ye shall receive."

"Boy, does that smell good," I chuckled as the aroma of Rosie's clam chowder filled the Modern Cabin. I couldn't help myself: I hustled over to the stove, lifted the lid, and took a good whiff.

"Now, that's what I call clam chowder," I drooled.

"Grab yourself a bowl and have some," Rosie replied. "It's ready." Yes, there is really nothing like a bowl of Rosie's clam chowder. I must have eaten half a dozen bowls of it. Each one better than the last. I felt as if I was going to burst.

"Don't forget," I mentioned to the crew who sat around the table. They were a well-fed, satisfied lot. "It's an early start tomorrow morning. If we're going to get a feed of walleye, we have to be up at dawn."

To my fishing partners, an early start was getting up at the crack of dawn. Well, the women felt that dawn was usually somewhere around noon, but not Les, our alarm clock. Les is a light sleeper and an early riser, a very early riser. He knows what the crack of dawn is; he greets it every morning.

At four-thirty the next morning, Les called. It was time to hit the lake and catch some wily walleye. Enough of getting up in time to fish for jackfish.

"I'm not going," Rosie called out. "I'm staying right here in bed. I'm not getting in that boat. I've had diarrhea all night."

"What do you think, Rosie?" I kidded. "Do you

148

think maybe you got a bad clam last night?"

"I don't know what I got, but I sure got something," she moaned unhappily.

There is something to be said for getting up early in the morning. It took the crew, minus Rosie of course, less than an hour to catch a limit of walleye and return to the lodge. Finally, I was able to throw fish up on the filleting table that didn't slime their way in fifty different directions at once. I whistled and sang, happy as a lark, while Les knocked the fillets off the walleye and I dug out the cheeks. Walleye cheeks are a very special little treat. Like filet mignon they are. Finally, after three days of fishing, we were going to have a real, honest-to-goodness fish fry. Walleye for breakfast—there was nothing better.

About the same time as the fish began to fry, the clouds returned, followed quickly by a steady drizzle. Before we finished eating a mess of walleye fillets, the winds picked up and the drizzle turned to a steady rain. It was then that Rosie spoke up.

"You know we've got to be out of this unit by noon," she said very matter-of-factly. Sort of as if it were common knowledge.

"What do you mean?" I asked. "We're not leaving until tomorrow."

"Well, they told us when we checked in, we could only have this unit for two nights," Rosie responded. "But they said not to worry, they'd find us something else for the last night."

"What do you mean, something else? There is nothing else. At least nothing else that I want to stay in." I was beginning to have terrible flashbacks of uncontrolled snoring. "If we can't stay here for the last night, then I vote that we pack up and go home," I stated quite firmly. After all, I'd had about all the rain and jackfish I needed for a while.

"No!" Martha chirped. "No, I don't want to go home. Not yet. I'll bet they got lots of cancellations with this rain. Let's go see what else they've got. I want to fish some more." Mar and Rosie charged out the door, through the hordes of mosquitoes, into the rain, and headed for the office. I sat down to watch the rain and await the break in the clouds or the girls' return, whichever came first.

The rain had turned into a torrential downpour. I watched the gusher of water streaming from the downspout. Sheets of water cascaded over the lips of the eavestroughs. The ground in front of the cabins was solid sand, sand where no water at all gathered, until now. Now a second lake was forming in the sand out in front of our Modern Cabin. The mosquitoes sought shelter from the driving rain, and despite the citrus candle and the mosquito coils burning in the windows, they blackened the screens. The future did not look good for walleye fishing.

"We're in luck. We can get into one of the Non-Modern Cabins," Mar sang out as she and Rosie waded across the widening second lake and sloshed through the door.

"What does 'Non-Modern' mean?" I asked suspiciously.

"It's almost like this cabin," she replied happily. Mar

really wanted to stay and have another go at fishing, any kind of fishing. Mar loves to fish. "Except there's no running water. That's all. But it's got everything else. Just no running water. We can do without running water for one night."

"What does that bad clam say, Rosie?" I inquired as to the state of her health. "What do you say, kiddo, can the bad clam take a night with no running water?"

"Well, I've still got diarrhea, if that's what you mean." She shot me a dirty look.

"Of course, you realize that no running water means no biffy. It's a long run to the public john if that clam starts acting up in the middle of the night. I vote that if we have to move, we go home. Who's with me?" I asked, looking for some agreement from my fishing buddies.

As soon as the rain let up just a little, Les and I started packing and hauling gear. Out the front door of the Modern Cabin, across the newly formed lake, straight into the Non-Modern Cabin. Walking through the door with the first load of supplies, I looked around.

Once again, I was greeted by the smell of citrus candles and mosquito coils. Rose had already been there. The war on the mosquitoes was relentless.

"Are we in the right cabin?" I asked.

"Yeah, why, what's wrong with it?" Mar snapped at me. "This is good enough for me. It's all we need for one night."

"Oh, nothing," I replied. "It's just that it looks a little more like Early Bush Shack, without the dirt floor. Oh look, isn't this cute?" I quipped. "They gave us a piece of cardboard with legs instead of a kitchen table. Hey, and how about this?" I chuckled, when I put some of our supplies in the cupboard. "Look Ma, no dishes."

"They don't supply dishes in the Non-Modern Cabins," Mar commented, as if everybody knew that. "You have to bring your own."

"I see. Well, isn't that nice. I thought they just didn't supply running water; now they don't supply dishes either. That's good." I smiled and started looking through all the cupboards.

"And look, there's no cutlery, no pots, no pans, no teakettle, and no coffee pot. By gosh, you're right. It looks like a clean sweep to me. There's absolutely nothing in here. I vote that we pack up and head for home. Who's with me?"

"Don't panic. I brought a coffee pot," Mar chimed in, quite happy with the Non-Modern Cabin. "We'll make do. We'll go and borrow some stuff from the restaurant."

"Yeah, but I don't drink coffee," I grumbled, resigning myself to the fact that we were staying.

"Close the door," Rose yelled.

"I closed it," I replied.

"Well, close it again," she said.

"It won't stay closed," I said and laughed. "There's something wrong with the latch; it doesn't work."

"Well, slide something against it. There's a million mosquitoes in here already. We'll be eaten alive tonight," Rosie replied.

Now, it's just a darn a good thing that I'm not claustrophobic. As soon as I walked into the lone bedroom, I was thankful for all the years I had spent in the log house on the stump farm.

"So, folks, tell me, are we all going to sleep in here, in this . . . Non-Modern Cabin?" I chuckled.

"There's lots of room," Mar responded cheerily. "I'm going to sleep on the floor in the kitchen. And someone else can sleep on the floor in the bedroom."

"With all the space in this room, I was just thinking that it's going to be pretty cozy in here tonight. If we didn't know each other before we went to bed, we certainly will before the night is very old." I laughed, and I threw my shaving kit on one of the two cots. That was the best I had to stake a claim with. I wasn't volunteering for the floor. What with all the weak bladders in the crew, I figured it would be better to step on than be stepped on.

"C'mon, Bob, let's have something to eat," Rosie said. "This place will look a lot better after you've had something to eat. Then we'll be ready to go fishing as soon as the rain stops. Les, light this stove. I want to make some coffee."

"Just turn it on, Rose. It lights by itself, you know," Les replied very knowledgeably.

"I've got it turned on," Rosie replied laughing, "but I don't think the pilot light is working." The smell of propane filled the kitchen.

Les walked over to the stove. He checked the knob and was satisfied that the propane was indeed on. He flipped open a book of matches, tore out a single match and struck it. The match had barely crossed the little scratchy surface, it hardly had time to ignite, let alone

153

flare, when the room was lit with a bright flash.

WOOOF, roared the huge orange flame that leapt from the top of the stove. The wooof was followed by the sound of shoes retreating on the lino floor as the party all bolted for the door. But before two steps were taken, the flame settled down onto the burner. Les stood there for a second with the match in his hand.

"You know, I think I'll have a piece of toast," Les said, as if nothing had happened.

"I hope it's not a gas toaster," I said laughing and once more started for the door.

"I'm sorry, but there's no toaster," Mar said. "The Non-Modern Cabin doesn't come with a toaster."

"I don't need a toaster," Les declared. "You see, I'm going to make my toast in the oven. Haven't you ever made toast in an oven?" he inquired, giving me a funny look.

"I try to avoid that if at all possible," I replied. As Les turned the knob and opened the oven, I inched towards the door. "I'd be surprised if the pilot light in the oven works either," I said and laughed. I kicked the box holding the door shut out of the way, and backed out the door into the rain, where I was immediately engulfed in a cloud of mosquitoes. Les got down on his knees to have a good look inside the oven.

"I wonder where you're supposed to light it," he commented as he searched the inside of the oven looking for a light. "Maybe it's that little round hole," he muttered to himself as the faint smell of propane gas once again could be detected in the room. The instant he struck the match and put it in the oven, there was a loud WHUMP as a ball of fire rolled around inside the oven. It was amazing that the stove was still intact, and so was Les. He had not lost a single eyebrow to either the wooof or the whump.

"There, the oven's on," Les called out triumphantly. "Now, would anyone else like a piece of toast?" he asked as he opened a loaf of bread.

"Shut the door!" Rosie yelled. "You're letting the mosquitoes in."

Standing outside in the rain and the mosquitoes, I held the door shut, but I was still able to follow the coffee- and toast-making.

"Who turned my coffee down?" Rosie asked above the hum of the mosquitoes and the pitter-patter of raindrops. I peeked back through the door at the top burner and, sure enough, the big flame was now a little flame. It was barely detectable under the coffee pot.

"Les, did you turn that burner down?" Rosie asked accusingly.

"No, I didn't," Les replied. And he took a couple of steps closer to the stove to inspect. "I didn't touch your burner. Look at it, it's still on high."

"Well, how come there's no heat, then?" Rosie demanded to know.

"Well, there's no heat in the oven either," Les replied as he examined the two slices of slowly drying bread.

"Let's see what happens if you turn the oven off," I offered from the safety of the great outdoors.

"Then my toast won't get done," Les replied.

Reluctantly, he shut off the oven and immediately the flame on the burner leapt to life.

"That's better," Rosie said. "Now we're cookin'!"

"There we go," I laughed. "It appears you can only use one portion of the stove at a time. That must be where the Non-Modern part comes in."

As dusk and the rain both fell on the Non-Modern Cabin, we found out that playing cards would also be a challenge. The single light bulb over the cardboard table struggled vainly but, try as it might, there were not enough rays to play cards with. So our little fishing crew roughing it in the Non-Modern Cabin decided that the day had been so strenuous that we should retire early. Sleeping arrangements had been decided on. Somehow, in this wilderness, the girls had managed to scrounge up a couple of extra mattresses and blankets. These were thrown on the floor. Mar claimed one of them and a portion of the floor in the kitchen. Rosie and the second mattress got the floor in the bedroom, between the two cots. Les and I had to tough it out on the cots.

"Mar," I called out from the bedroom, where I stood looking at my cot. "You'll have to go over to the office again and tell them that the cleaning lady forgot to make the beds. In fact, she forgot to leave any sheets or blankets. There's only this thin thing that looks like a mattress cover on my cot."

"I'm sorry," she laughed. "These cabins don't come with any bedding. You have to bring your own."

"But you've got a blanket," I whined.

"They made an exception for us when I told them

Rose and I were going to be sleeping on the floor," she replied.

"You've got to be kidding me," I snarled, thinking of my down-filled sleeping bags at home. "We should have gone home like I suggested," I grumbled as I crawled in under the mattress cover.

There was barely enough room for Rosie and her mattress on the floor between the two cots. I watched with more than casual interest as she entered the room. She crawled in on the mattress, and curled up like a pretzel under her blanket.

"How's that bad clam of yours tonight, Rosie?" I asked and laughed.

I thought Les was already asleep, but apparently not. He let out a howl of laughter.

"Never mind my clam," Rosie snapped. "You just worry about yourself."

"Well, as a matter of fact, I am. I'm worried about that bad clam and about myself as well, Rosie," I replied. "After all, you've had diarrhea all day, and right now, the way you're curled up there, you've got that thing pointing right at me. There's not very much between the bad clam and me, should that thing start working overtime tonight. Why don't you turn the other way and aim at Les?"

"I'll aim whichever way I want," she growled at me.

I lay there in the dark, in my Jockey shorts under the thin mattress cover, listening to the sounds of the night. The sound of the wind whistling through the trees. The soothing pitter-pattering of the rain on the roof. The hum of the mosquitoes swarming the windows. The

157

eerie buzz of the few mosquitoes who had persevered and were now in the room with us. Having hounded us all day, they now filled the dark, searching incessantly for a place to land and drill for blood. Then the unmistakable, not-so-soothing rattle of snoring began. It gained strength, until it resounded throughout the building, drowning out all other sounds.

In the dark, my senses honed, I could detect the smells in the air. The smell of moisture from the rain and the lake, heavy in the air, was refreshing. However, there were other smells, competing smells. The scent of the citrus candle, burning in the darkness, wafted throughout the Not-So-Modern Cabin, mixed with the ever-present smell of smouldering mosquito coils.

Then the bad clam that had haunted Rosie for the past twenty-four hours again made its presence known. The first burst caused me to duck under the mattress cover. Then another odour wafted through the room, mingling with the smell of the citrus candle and the mosquito coil. Man, if the smell from that fart doesn't kill the mosquitoes, nothing will, I moaned to myself. Rosie was going to have to check her bed in the morning, I thought. One couldn't take that many chances with a bad clam.

Finally, I looked at my watch; two-thirty and I hadn't slept a wink. Slowly I dragged my sorry butt, clad in my Jockey shorts, out of bed. I stepped gingerly over Rosie and in the dark managed to sidestep Mar as I made my way to the door. I moved the door-stopper box to one side, and quietly, I slipped out for some fresh air and a much-needed leak. Outside, the rain was still falling and the mosquitoes still biting. Absent-mindedly, I let go of the door handle.

CLICK.

I heard the unmistakable sound of the door latch snapping shut as I stood in the rain in front of the Non-Modern Cabin. I looked around to see who had joined me. No one. That was strange. When I finished feeding the mosquitoes outside, I confronted the door. It was still closed. Closed and locked. For once, the door that wouldn't stay closed all day had, all by itself, locked me out. In the rain, with only my shorts on. It was decision time. Should I bang on the door to the snoring, smell-infested cabin and wake up the crew, or head for my van? I could only thank the guy who invented the keyless entry system. I ran for my van.

From the back seat, I pulled out my floater coat. I reclined the driver's seat to a horizontal position and pulled the coat over me. I squirmed around under the coat for some time trying to get warm and comfortable. I pulled my feet up under me and lay there. I squashed a lone mosquito who had dared to invade my privacy. The pitter-patter of falling rain was like music to my ears. I took a deep breath of the fresh, rain-filled air and I soon drifted off.

Sometime today, we would be going home.

"IT'S ONLY AN ELEPHANT!"

"Hey," snarled the guy who got out of the black pickup truck with a camper on the back. The greeting was followed by a string of foreign words that I could not understand, but I guessed they were not very complimentary.

"I beg your pardon," I replied. "Are you talking to me?"

"Yes," he replied with a thick accent. "What is the matter with your wife? She almost rammed into my truck."

Oh boy, I thought, this is going to be the perfect end to a great day.

Mar and I were somewhere in the middle of the Hwange National Park in Zimbabwe when the fun and games started. We were on one of our daily expeditions, a safari, looking at African wildlife. Elephants, zebras, giraffes, cape buffalo, and a variety of rainbow-coloured birds had paraded before us on this day.

Like most of the roads in the park, the one we were on was a simple tar road, eight feet wide. There was enough room for one vehicle at a time. The rules of the road were quite simple: If you met another vehicle, you kept the right-hand wheels on the tar road. The left-hand wheels, and the passenger, travelled in the grass — or what we prairie people would call the ditch. The whole driving thing in Zimbabwe required a considerable amount of concentration. People there drive on the left-hand side — to my mind, the wrong side — of the road. It was difficult to remember that the driver was always supposed to be in the centre of the road.

"Keep one wheel on the road, and the other in the grass," we had been told. This worked very well in theory; however, the grass along many of the roads in Hwange National Park was not normal grass. It was elephant grass, ten to twelve feet high, that towered over the White Princess like a jillion tall, skinny trees. Although it was a rare occurrence, we did meet other vehicles. These drivers were mostly foreigners, such as we, and we usually slowed to a halt — sometimes both vehicles sitting with the left wheels in the grass, each waiting for the other to move forward.

"Don't go in there!" I shouted to Mar, as the left-hand wheels of the White Princess and I, the passenger, edged into the tall grass. Mar was driving the White Princess and I was driving her crazy. She was having no problem dealing with the narrow road or the elephant grass, but, in my opinion, she was taking the corners a little too close, approaching each as if she were expecting a truck to come roaring around it. The left-hand side of the car, and I, seemed to be going deeper and deeper into the tall elephant grass with every corner.

"What's the matter?" she asked and yanked the White Princess back onto the narrow strip of tar.

"You don't know what's in that tall grass," I snorted. "This is ridiculous. That bloody park warden told me this was short-grass savannah, loaded with animals. Look at this stuff. You can't see six inches into it. We could be within feet—hell, inches!—of elephants, lions, rhinos, anything and we wouldn't see a bloody thing. You know, Mar, everything in the grass there is bigger than the White Princess. If we hit something in that grass, we'll feed the lions tonight."

It was in just that kind of setting—eight feet of winding tar road lined by twelve-foot elephant grass—when it happened. Mar was driving, and I was giving unsolicited instructions. She was cruising right along, with all the confidence of a Saskatchewan girl. She coasted around a corner and instantly slammed on the brakes. There, right in the middle of the road, stood a humongous bull elephant.

Now, seeing an elephant was not a new occurrence. We had seen hundreds of elephants: elephants crossing the road, elephants sauntering down the road ahead of us, elephants in the ditch, elephants at the pans, and elephants on the plains. It was safe to say that there were elephants everywhere. But this elephant, he was, well . . . he was huge.

"There's . . . there's an elephant on the road!" Mar exclaimed.

"Yeah," I replied. "A bull. And he's a biggie."

"What should I do?" she asked.

"Wait, don't move until I get the camera. This guy's huge, and I want to get some shots of him. Then you can just pull up a little for some good close-up shots," I replied.

"But he's just standing there, staring at me," she replied. "Maybe I should back up."

"It's only an elephant," I laughed. "Let me get some pictures." By now, I had the big bull in the viewfinder. He was a magnificent beast; the entire viewfinder was filled with his enormous presence.

"Drive up a bit," I coaxed. "I want to get an action shot. Maybe even a shot of him walking into the grass."

"Are you crazy?" Mar asked. "I'm not driving up there."

As others had done, the big bull turned slightly, and very slowly and deliberately, he started to walk off the road. It was a great picture. I had to marvel at how an animal that big could walk into the tall grass and disappear right before your eyes. But the big bull didn't disappear. Well, not completely, anyway. Sticking out of the tall grass and protruding over the road was this huge ear. The ear slowly fanned, back and forth, into the grass, then over the road.

"You can drive on now," I said to Mar as the camera rolled. "C'mon, let's move it. Maybe I can get another shot before he disappears into the grass."

"But he's still there," she protested. "I can still see

part of him. I'm not going to drive up there until I know he's gone."

"C'mon, it's only an elephant, Mar," I replied. "And a gentleman at that. Look, he's stepped off the road to allow you drive on by."

"No way," she stated quite firmly. "I'm not driving up there."

At that moment, the huge ear fanned back out over the road and brought with it a huge trunk that was waving from side to side.

"He's coming," Mar whispered. "He's coming after us."

"Naw, he's probably just taking a peek to see if the road's clear now," I chuckled.

"Bull," Mar replied as she fumbled with the gearshift and the White Princess began to rock and roll.

"What are you doing?" I asked. "You're buggering up my picture."

"I'm getting out of here," she declared.

As she spoke, more of the elephant appeared from out of the tall grass. Now I could see the trunk plainly, swinging from side to side, and two ears fanning. Actually, I think the movement of the elephant emerging from the grass gave the ears a distorted look. They were sticking straight out from his head. The big bull elephant looked as if he had enjoyed as much of this game as he could stand. He wasn't standing it anymore. The rest of the huge carcass had left the grass. Now he was coming straight at us.

"I think he wants a closer look," I said to Mar. "Why don't you just drive up there and scare him?"

"Scare him. You run up there and scare him," Mar stated. "I'm scared enough for the both of us. I'm out of here, right now."

"Where are you going?" I kidded.

"I'm backing up. Where did you think I was going?"

The White Princess was vibrating and shaking wildly. The big bull elephant was slowly and deliberately walking toward us. It was becoming clear to me that the White Princess was hardly a match for a slow deliberate-stepping bull elephant.

"Bob, I can't get this thing into reverse," Mar complained. There was a note of urgency in her voice.

More and more elephant filled the viewfinder as the bull elephant steadily advanced. Even through the viewfinder, the massive trunk was swinging violently from side to side. Out one side of the viewfinder it went, back it came across the width of the lens, then back out the other side. The huge ears were fanning angrily. That big bull elephant was right ticked off and getting mighty close, too close. Mar had both hands on the gearshift and was frantically trying to jam it into reverse. She had the gas pedal pushed to the floor, and the White Princess was vibrating wildly as the elephant drew closer. Mar was just a tad worried.

"I can't get this bloody thing into reverse!" Mar wailed.

"Just push the gearshift to the left and pull it back," I replied. The elephant was still coming.

"I am," she said. The knob on the gearshift must have resembled a pinball machine as Mar worked frantically to find reverse.

Keeping the advancing elephant in the viewfinder, I decided it was time to help. I reached over and grabbed the gearshift. I pulled it toward me, then jammed it back.

"There," I pronounced, "it's in reverse."

The motor roared. The White Princess reacted immediately. She seemed to jump, forward, right at the advancing big bull elephant.

"Oops, sorry," I apologized. "Wrong gear."

This boldness on the part of the little White Princess surprised the big bull elephant. His eyes seemed to grow wider, rounder. He tossed his head into the air. He lifted his trunk and flapped his ears. He hesitated for only a split second, then he moved forward again.

"Oh, cripes," Mar moaned as she grabbed the gearshift. Once again, there was more vibrating and jiggling as she fought with the gearshift.

Suddenly, the White Princess jerked and jumped. Backwards. Finally, Mar had succeeded in finding reverse. With a sputter and a cough, the White Princess jumped, then started back. The elephant continued to advance. Then, without warning, Mar jammed on the brakes.

"What's the matter now?" I asked.

"I can't go back any farther," Mar stated.

"Why not?" I asked. The big bull was once more getting to be awfully large in the viewfinder.

"Some idiot has stopped right behind me," she complained.

I turned around and looked. Sure enough, right in the center of the tar road, about fifty feet behind the

White Princess, sat a black truck with a camper on it. The driver was leaning out the window. He, too, had a video camera. And he, too, was filming the big bull elephant.

"Back up," I yelled and waved for him to back up or get out of the way. He stayed where he was, leaning out the window. I looked back at the big elephant. Now he was really close.

"Back up, you idiot," I yelled again.

"He won't move," Mar replied.

"Gun it then," I yelled. "Ram the fool."

"What'll happen if I hit him?" she asked.

"Then maybe he'll know enough to get out of the way," I replied.

Slowly Mar started to back up, but the black truck just sat there. The driver was more interested in filming the advancing elephant than moving out of the way.

"Hit it!" I yelled. "Drive that sucker right in the nose!"

And Mar did. She gunned the motor, the White Princess jumped and, as fast as it would go in reverse, sped towards the black truck. That got the driver's attention. The idiot scrambled to get back into his seat. All of him, that is, except his right arm and the camera. He wasn't taking any chances on missing the shot that might qualify him for Picture of the Year. The black truck obviously had more power than the White Princess. It easily pulled away from us, putting ample distance between the two vehicles.

The big bull elephant was still far too close to us. The black truck led the way. Down the tar road we backed, around the first bend and out of sight of the elephant. Well, almost out of sight: The tops of the big, fanning ears and the trunk waving around in the air like a periscope were still visible above the tall grass. It appeared that the big bull elephant still wanted a piece of the White Princess.

Back around another corner we went until the elephant was completely out of sight. Finally Mar stopped the vehicle, but she did not take her eyes off the tar road and the twelve-foot elephant grass.

"I don't think I'd take it out of reverse," I cautioned her. "Just in case."

Good decision, for it wasn't long before the waving trunk and the fanning ears appeared over the grass. The big bull elephant was still advancing.

The chase lasted for over a mile. Then, suddenly, just as if there had never been anything on the tar road except the White Princess and the black truck with the camper on it, the big bull elephant disappeared. He was gone. Vanished. Into thin air, or into tall grass.

"Do you think it's safe to go?" Mar asked.

"I'm not sure it's safe to take this thing out of reverse," I replied. "You may never get it back in again."

We waited. But there was no sign of the big bull elephant. It was a very skeptical Mar who finally slid the gearshift out of reverse and into low gear. Slowly she moved the car forward. The black truck with the camper on the back followed. The driver continued to hold his camera out the window. Cautiously, Mar inched around each bend in the road. When we reached a point where we thought we had last seen the big bull elephant, Mar gunned the engine. The White Princess literally shot along the tar road, through the tall grass, towards safety. The black truck with the camper on the back stayed right on our tail.

When we reached a game-viewing stand at one of the pans (watering holes), Mar pulled in for a well-deserved rest. We were just walking up the steps when the black truck pulled in behind us.

"Hey," snarled the guy who got out of the black pickup truck with a camper on the back. The greeting was followed by a string of foreign words that I could not understand, but I guessed they were not very complimentary.

"I beg your pardon," I replied. "Are you talking to me?"

"Yes," he replied with a thick accent. "What is the matter with your wife? She almost rammed into my truck."

Oh, boy, I thought, this is going to be the perfect end to a great day.

"Listen, buddy," I replied to the guy as I halted my climb up the steps leading to the game-watching platform. "What's the matter with my wife? What's the matter with *you*? Why didn't you back up?"

"Because I was taking pictures of the elephant," came the reply in the thick accent.

"Didn't you realize that it was us who were in danger?" I asked. "We could have been stepped on. Killed."

"Oh yes. I know," he replied. "I know that.

169

Yesterday, a little car just like yours was crushed by an elephant. I saw it. The father, he ran away and hid in the trees. But the little girl, she did not get out of the car. She was killed."

"And you still sat there and didn't move?" I asked.

"I was taking the pictures," he argued. "I didn't get any pictures yesterday and I wanted to get the pictures today. I would have liked to get the pictures of the elephant stepping on your car," he replied.

"But we could have been killed," I said. "Didn't you think of that?'

"Oh yes," he replied. Then his face got very serious. He looked me square in the eye and said very seriously, "You know, you should be more careful."

"JUST TAKE CARRY-ON"

"By the way, hon, I got you a ticket, too," Mar advised me one afternoon.

"Me?" I replied. This was an unexpected change of events. The annual trip to Vegas had been planned for several weeks. Every fall, Mar and her sister Rita met in Vegas for a little get-together. The telephone lines had been very busy, humming and buzzing between Edmonton and Victoria as the great day approached and the last-minute touches were finalized.

"Me? You . . . you're kidding?" I stammered. This was somewhat of a pleasant surprise. "You mean, I get to go and share in your weekend getaway?" I could not really believe my ears, for the annual Vegas venture was normally a trip that included only the girls.

"Hon, do you by chance need someone to carry your suitcase?" I asked sarcastically.

"Pack light," Mar replied, ignoring my smart remark. "Just take a carry-on. That's all you need."

"Why's that?" I asked. A normal question, for it seemed that whenever we neared an airport, I was loaded down with suitcases and assorted bags.

"If you only take a carry-on, you don't have to wait for your bags," she informed me. "Then you can walk right onto one of the tour buses. That's what I've been doing every time I go. It saves a lot of hassle in the airport."

"Is that right? I didn't know that tour buses stopped at the Jockey Club," I commented. "When did they start that?"

"No, they've never stopped at the Jockey Club. We just get off at the Aladdin, and walk across the street."

I don't mind admitting that I was absolutely amazed as we left the house carrying only two small bags for a four-day, three-night stay in Vegas. We zipped into the long-term parking area. I carried the two little bags. I smiled to myself as I hoisted the light load. This was a far cry from the load of suitcases, bags, and parcels that the old workhorse, Pack Mule Bob, normally carried to the check-in counter. We whisked through the check-in so fast, I hardly knew we were there. We breezed through US Customs and sailed on through security. In no time flat, we were sitting in the waiting room. I could only shake my head at the simplicity of the exercise. There was no doubt about it, Mar had this carry-on bit down to a T. Everything certainly ran smoother than it ever had in the past.

When they called our flight, I sashayed down the

ramp like I was on a stroll in the park. I even had time to kibitz with the stewardess. I flipped the carry-on bags into the overhead racks and sat down. My feet slid in under the seat ahead of me and, for the first time, I realized there really was room down there.

"Why haven't we done this in the past?" I asked.

"What do you mean?" she replied. "This is how I always go to Vegas. It's much simpler when you only take one carry-on bag, isn't it?"

"It certainly is," I agreed. "It looks like I'll even have time to read the morning paper. I got to hand it to you, Mar, you've got this baby aced," I congratulated her as I settled back and buried my nose in the paper.

"Those passengers who purchased Air Only tickets can claim their bags at Carousel 2 on the Arrivals level," announced the voice over the intercom as the plane was landing in Vegas.

"Not us," I chuckled to Mar. "We got carry-on." Man, but the time had just flown. It seemed as if we had just boarded and now we were landing.

"Those passengers who have purchased the Full Holiday Package may proceed directly to one of the tour buses parked outside the doors on the Arrivals level. A tour guide will meet you in the airport and escort you to the buses. Your baggage will be delivered directly to your hotel room."

"Did . . . uh, did we buy the Full Holiday Package?" I asked.

"Ssshhh . . . just a minute," she whispered. "I want to hear which bus we have to get on."

"Those passengers going to the MGM, Bally's, the

173

Maxim or the Imperial Palace, take Tour Bus 2. Those going . . . " the voice droned on. Finally, the last bus and the final destination were announced.

"It doesn't sound like they're stopping at the Aladdin," I mentioned to Mar.

"We'll take Bus 2 and get off at Bally's," she replied without a hint of concern.

"Don't they check your tickets, or something?" I asked.

"They never check anything," she replied.

"Well, what happens if they do check?" I inquired. Somewhere down deep in the pit of my stomach, I could feel the butterflies. They were starting to flap their wings. Suddenly, I began to have second thoughts. Maybe this carry-on trip wasn't all it appeared to be.

"Don't worry," she warbled. "They never check anything. They just want your money. They're so happy to see you, they just welcome you to Vegas and stuff like that." Mar is one cool cat when she wants to be.

Leaving the airplane and the trek through the airport were almost like every other trip. Almost, but not quite. For the first time, I was not laden with three hundred pounds of baggage. Mar led the way. Down the aisle, up the ramp and into the terminal she strode. Mar was no stranger to the Las Vegas airport. She whisked through the Arrivals terminal, down past the Baggage Claim area and out onto the street. I was right behind her, hot on her heels, and — lucky me! — I got to lug both carry-on bags. This part of the trip certainly had a familiar ring to it. Unencumbered, I zipped right along behind her. I whipped through the crowd, dodging and sidestepping people. The carry-ons were a breeze, they were no problem whatsoever. But I had to hustle, or I would have been left behind. Mar waited for no one.

Outside the gates, Mar had no difficulty at all finding tour bus number 2, our transportation to the Jockey Club, via Bally's of course. Mar bounded through the door, past the driver and the tour guide, right to the middle of the tour bus. She picked a choice seat, next to the window, and settled in as if she owned it. Me and my butterflies, on the other hand, were slinking along behind her, crawling down the aisle, hoping that no one had seen us.

I was having a terrible struggle over what I should do about the carry-ons. I wasn't sure if I should put them up in the overhead, shove them under the seat in front of me, or keep them on my lap. I chose the overhead. As soon as I sat down, I cursed the decision. If I was going to have to run for it, I didn't want to lose my carry-ons. I should have kept them on my lap.

"Welcome, welcome, welcome," sang out the elderly tour guide. "Welcome to Las Vegas." Although he had yet to take his eyes off the paper he was reading, he did appear to be enjoying his lot in life. He took up a position at the front of the bus, where he continued with his greeting.

"Is everyone enjoying themselves so far?" he asked. He wore a huge smile, although it seemed a little strained as he fumbled with the stack of paper that someone had pushed on him. It was no big deal, but he was mumbling to himself as he fought his way through the mess, trying to find a starting point.

"Looks like it's his first day on the job," I whispered to Mar. But she had other things on her mind, like reading some nondescript piece of paper she had picked up on the dash through the airport. She ignored me.

"Oh yes," said the old fellow. Obviously he had just found the right page.

"Is . . . is there anyone on this bus who has paid for the Air Only portion of the package? This . . . this bus is only for those who have purchased the Full Holiday Package," advised the happy tour guide. Repeating the message we had received on the plane seemed to be the first item in the package of material he had been fighting to sort out. After the announcement, he stood at the front of the bus, looking at the rows of faces looking back at him.

"Good. Good," he sang out while he put page one to the bottom of the stack.

With the second page now at the top of the pile, he strolled through the bus counting the passengers. He smiled and greeted each person. He pointed to each head, ensuring an accurate count, then stepped forward to count the next. There were only two other people sitting in the seats behind the ones Mar had chosen for us. I watched the smile fade from the old tour guide's face when he arrived at our seats. His hands began to shake when he finished pointing to our heads. He stopped counting and stared at the two people seated near the back of the bus, then down at page two. Something did not add up. There were more heads than there were names on the page. He shook his head; then, muttering to himself, he slowly turned around and dragged his poor old body back to the front of the bus. Suddenly he looked like a man who was not enjoying his first day on the job. It must be a tour guide's worst fear, too many heads on the bus. The look on his face told me that he knew things were about to get worse.

I started to sweat, for I, too, knew that things could only get worse. The butterflies were no longer just fluttering their wings. They were really stirring things up, flapping like crazy. I could feel the little beads of water forming on my brow and under my arms.

"Man, it's hot in here. Why don't they turn on the air conditioning? Don't you find it hot in here?" I whispered to Mar.

"Relax," she whispered. "The air conditioning is on." Mar continued to read the little piece of paper.

"Is . . . is there anyone on this bus who . . . who only paid for the air portion of their trip?" asked a sad-looking tour guide whose voice had just picked up a noticeable quaver. "This bus is for those who purchased the Full Holiday Package only," the old tour guide repeated. His hands were shaking so hard now that he could hardly hold his instruction papers, let alone read them.

The passengers all sat tight in their seats, looking back at him. All except Mar, who was still busy reading the fine print on her piece of paper. Things had not got better for the old gent.

"I've . . . I've got two people too many on this bus!" he wailed, and scanned the bus waiting for someone, anyone, to stand up and get off the bus.

177

Still no one moved. "He's going to narrow this down and kick our sorry butts off here," I whispered to Mar, but I might as well have been on another planet. She ignored me. I could feel more perspiration, the heat was rising, I was sweating all over my body.

"Look, the rest of the buses have already left," I mumbled in Mar's ear to make sure she heard me. I had to be about as nervous as the old tour guide. No, I was past nervous, I was scared. I always thought that going to Las Vegas was supposed to be a fun time. This was anything but fun. I was ready to bolt for the door, but the old tour guide stood between me and my freedom. I knew that, sooner or later, I was going to have to get off the bus. I felt like a criminal, a prisoner on a bloody tour bus. The only way off was through the old guy. If I made a dash for it and gave it my all, I could run right over top of him. But where was I going to go then? Outside, there were more people, and some of them wore uniforms and guns. Man, I knew enough about guns and the trigger-happy Yanks. So I sat and I died a thousand deaths on that tour bus, my prison.

Mar, however, was as cool as a cucumber, and she was not about to move.

"Let me try this," the old guide's voice cracked into the microphone. "How many people are going to the MGM?"

Two people held up their hands.

"That's right," he declared. I could see just the trace of a smile ripple across his trembling lips. "Now . . . now how many are going to Bally's?" The old fellow was gaining a little confidence; there was renewed strength in his voice. It was beginning to sound a little more authoritative.

Five people held up their hands.

"Is that one or two people, sir?" he asked, looking directly at me.

He's got us, I thought. My heart was pounding in my throat and I looked at Mar, who still had her nose buried in the piece of paper. She ignored him as she did me. Since my hand was one of the five in the air, and Mar's was still clutching her piece of paper, I meekly held up two fingers.

"Thank you, sir," said the old tour guide. He was smiling now, but not for long. I watched, and swallowed hard, as he glanced down at a sheet of paper. I saw the smile fade. I swear I could see the worry lines growing deeper.

"Now . . . now I've got two people too many going to Bally's!" The old guy almost cried. "Please, folks," he said, and his hands were shaking so hard that I thought he was going to drop the pile of papers he held in his hands. "Please, it's for your own good. If you've got Air Only tickets, your suitcases will be left at the airport. You'll lose your suitcases."

Not us, I sweated, our suitcases are only carry-ons. They were right here on the bus with us, tucked neatly in the overhead. Again, I cursed my decision. On my lap they would have been ready for a rapid exit. Mar's eyes never left her piece of paper.

"Okay then," the tired old tour guide mumbled into the mike.

"Uh-oh," I whispered to Mar. "This is it. He's got it

narrowed down to six people now. This is where he gets us." There's a first time for everything, I thought, and this will be the first time I've ever been booted off a tour bus. The air-conditioned bus was hot and clammy. Now, waiting for the hammer to fall, I was sweating like a stuck hog. I sat back and closed my eyes, waiting for the inevitable.

"Okay," his voice was almost a whisper. "Oh . . . Yes . . . Welcome to Las Vegas and . . . enjoy your holiday." With those final remarks, he turned and stumbled off the bus.

I was still sitting on the edge of my seat, wiping my sweaty palms on my trousers when the tour bus pulled away from the terminal.

"I told you it would be okay," Mar smiled, looking up from her paper. "I always ride the tour buses. They never check you."

The first stop was the MGM. There were no tour guides outside to meet the two guests who departed. The bus driver pointed the way to the entrance of the hotel.

"Enjoy your stay, folks," he offered.

At the second stop, Bally's, things were different. I could see two tour guides. They stood out like sore thumbs. Both were standing by the sidewalk, like Wal-Mart greeters, waiting for the four guests and two freeloaders to depart.

From the middle of the bus, we should have been the last two to depart, as the other four guests of Bally's were seated ahead of us. I was only half right. When I stood up to get the carry-ons from the overhead, Mar was up and out of her seat like a shot.

For some strange reason those two little bags were reluctant to leave the overhead, they were giving me just a wee bit of trouble. While I struggled to remove them, Mar blew past me and raced through the bus. One passenger from the front row just barely nosed her out of being the first one off the bus.

I was dead meat, left on the bus to struggle with two carry-ons. A very patient driver waited while I pulled the carry-ons from the overhead rack. Then I raced for the door. Suddenly those two little bags felt like large suitcases packed to the seams. I think I bumped, banged, and slammed those carry-on bags into every seat and all the remaining passengers in my haste to flee. Finally, I stumbled off the bus, in last place.

Out on the sidewalk, I paused and looked around. I saw the two tour guides, one by the bus, the other up near the hotel doors. I saw the four legitimate riders, all walking towards the doors. All carrying nothing. But I couldn't see Mar. I was surprised to find that she was not waiting for me. I took a second look at the tour guides and the other passengers, but Mar was nowhere to be seen. Mar had vanished.

Panic. Panic set in. My first thought was that the worst had happened. Mar had been nabbed.

"This way, sir," I heard a voice call out from the direction of the hotel door and my heart sank. This is it, I thought, as another burst of sweat streamed from my pores. I looked up to see the tour guide near the hotel door. She was waving at me, gesturing for me to come forth. But I was already sixth, and that was too many.

Frantically I scanned the area, searching for Mar.

"Where did she get to?" I muttered.

Then I spotted her. She was a good half-block away, walking casually along the side of the hotel. She was leaving the area as if nothing had happened, heading for the Strip.

Without acknowledging the tour guide, I deliberately, but hastily, made an about-face. Then with all the grace of a pack mule, I strolled (well, maybe I ran a little) after Mar.

"That's the last time I pack a carry-on," I grumbled as I strode past her, in my haste to put as much distance as possible between myself and the tour guides. "Next time, you can do what you want, but I'm taking a suitcase and a taxi."

"Oh, you worry too much," came her flippant answer as she rushed to keep up.

"No wonder I've got bleeding ulcers," I moaned as I hurried for the safety of the Jockey Club.

ROBERT J. (BOB) ADAMS

Bob Adams was born in Turner Valley, Alberta in 1938. He grew up in the Edson area, in a log house, built by his father on a farm rich in swamp spruce, tamarack, willows and muskeg.

Bob, an avid outdoorsman, was one of the fortunate few who was able to live his boyhood dreams as he entered the workforce. In 1960, after a number of years with the Alberta Forest Service and Royal Canadian Mounted Police, he began a career with the Provincial Government as a Fish and Wildlife Officer. For the next 33 years, he found his homes to include Brooks, Strathmore, Hinton, Calgary, Peace River and Edmonton.

In 1993, after a full career in Enforcement, he retired from Fish and Wildlife and wrote his first book, The Stump Farm. Today, Bob resides in Edmonton, Alberta with his wife Martha where he continues to work on his writing.

GIVE A "ROBERT J. ADAMS" BOOK TO A FRIEND

Megamy Publishing Ltd.
Box 3507
Spruce Grove, AB   T7X 3A7

Send to:

Name:_____

Street:_____

City:_____
Province/   Postal/
State:_____ Zip Code:_____

Please send:

"The Stump Farm"   @ $14.95 = _____
"Beyond the Stump Farm"   @ $14.95 = _____
"Horse Cop"   @ $15.95 = _____
"Fish Cop"   @ $15.95 = _____
"The Elephant's Trunk"   @ $15.95 = _____
Shipping and handling per book   @ $ 4.00 = _____
                                  7% GST   = _____
                    Total amount enclosed: _____

Make cheque or money order payable to:
Megamy Publishing Ltd.
Price subject to change without prior notice.
ORDERS OUTSIDE OF CANADA must be paid in U.S. funds by
cheque or money order drawn on U.S. or Canadian Bank.
Sorry no C.O.D.'s.

Gift from:
Name:_____
Address:_____
City:_____
Province/   Postal/
State:_____Zip Code:_____

Megamy Publishing will gladly enclose your personal
message with each book sent as a gift.

GIVE A "ROBERT J. ADAMS" BOOK TO A FRIEND

Megamy Publishing Ltd.
Box 3507
Spruce Grove, AB   T7X 3A7

Send to:

Name:_____

Street:_____

City:_____

Province/   Postal/
State:_____ Zip Code:_____

Please send:

"The Stump Farm"   @ $14.95 = _____
"Beyond the Stump Farm"   @ $14.95 = _____
"Horse Cop"   @ $15.95 = _____
"Fish Cop"   @ $15.95 = _____
"The Elephant's Trunk"   @ $15.95 = _____
Shipping and handling per book @ $ 4.00 = _____
                              7% GST   = _____
              Total amount enclosed: _____

Make cheque or money order payable to:
Megamy Publishing Ltd.
Price subject to change without prior notice.
ORDERS OUTSIDE OF CANADA must be paid in U.S. funds by
cheque or money order drawn on U.S. or Canadian Bank.
Sorry no C.O.D.'s.

Gift from:
Name:_____
Address:_____
City:_____
Province/   Postal/
State:_____ Zip Code:_____

Megamy Publishing will gladly enclose your personal
message with each book sent as a gift.

GIVE A "ROBERT J. ADAMS" BOOK TO A FRIEND

Megamy Publishing Ltd.
Box 3507
Spruce Grove, AB   T7X 3A7

Send to:

Name:_____

Street:_____

City:_____

Province/   Postal/
State:_____ Zip Code:_____

Please send:

"The Stump Farm"	@ $14.95 =	_____
"Beyond the Stump Farm"	@ $14.95 =	_____
"Horse Cop"	@ $15.95 =	_____
"Fish Cop"	@ $15.95 =	_____
"The Elephant's Trunk"	@ $15.95 =	_____
Shipping and handling per book	@ $ 4.00 =	_____
	7% GST =	_____
	Total amount enclosed:	_____

Make cheque or money order payable to:
Megamy Publishing Ltd.
Price subject to change without prior notice.
ORDERS OUTSIDE OF CANADA must be paid in U.S. funds by
cheque or money order drawn on U.S. or Canadian Bank.
Sorry no C.O.D.'s.

Gift from:
Name:_____
Address:_____
City:_____
Province/   Postal/
State:_____ Zip Code:_____

Megamy Publishing will gladly enclose your personal
message with each book sent as a gift.

Megamy Publishing Ltd.
Box 3507
Spruce Grove, AB   T7X 3A7

Send to:
Name:_____

Street:_____

City:_____
Province/   Postal/
State:_____ Zip Code:_____

Please send:

"The Stump Farm"	@ $14.95 =	_____
"Beyond the Stump Farm"	@ $14.95 =	_____
"Horse Cop"	@ $15.95 =	_____
"Fish Cop"	@ $15.95 =	_____
"The Elephant's Trunk"	@ $15.95 =	_____
Shipping and handling per book	@ $ 4.00 =	_____
	7% GST =	_____
	Total amount enclosed:	_____

Make cheque or money order payable to:
Megamy Publishing Ltd.
Price subject to change without prior notice.
ORDERS OUTSIDE OF CANADA must be paid in U.S. funds by
cheque or money order drawn on U.S. or Canadian Bank.
Sorry no C.O.D.'s.

Gift from:
Name:_____
Address:_____
City:_____
Province/   Postal/
State:_____ Zip Code:_____

Megamy Publishing will gladly enclose your personal
message with each book sent as a gift.